# MAVERICK SEA FARE

SKETCHES AND TEXT
BY DEE CARSTARPHEN

PUBLISHED BY PEN AND INK PRESS
DISTRIBUTED BY BANYAN BOOKS, INC.
P. O. BOX 431160, MIAMI, FLA. 33143
(305) 665-6011

PRINTED BY SOUTHEASTERN PRINTING INC., STUART, FLORIDA

# TABLE of CONTENTS

**VIRGIN ISLANDS**

IN THE OLDEN DAYS, VISITORS SAMPLING FOOD IN THE CARIBBEAN FOUND IT GENERALLY UNINTERESTING. IN SPITE OF THE ABUNDANCE OF FRESH FRUITS AND ROOTS, FISH AND VEGETABLES, FOOD FROM THE DAYS OF SLAVERY WAS GENERALLY DULL. FISH, CORN- MEAL MUSH (FUNGI) AND RICE WITH HOT SAUCE POURED INDISCRIMINATELY OVER ALL. THE LAST FEW YEARS HAVE SEEN A MAJOR CHANGE IN THE COOKING OVER THE WHOLE CARIBBEAN AREA. EACH SECTION HAS DEVELOPED ITS OWN DISHES WITH SOMETHING OF INTEREST FOR EVERYONE — DUTCH, FRENCH AND INDIAN INFLUENCES MINGLE AND BLEND. THE ADVENT OF TOURISM AND THE EXTRA MONEY IT BRINGS — THE SHRINKING OF THE WORLD DUE TO FASTER TRANSPORTATION — WHATEVER THE REASON, THERE ARE NOW LOTS OF GOOD THINGS TO COOK AND EAT IN THE CARIBBEAN.

THIS BOOK WANTS TO SHARE SOME OF THE IDEAS AND INFORMATION DISCOVERED DURING YEARS OF SAILING THROUGH THE ISLANDS — AND HOPES TO GIVE A SMALL TASTE AND FEELING OF THE REAL WAY TO EXPERIENCE THIS SPECIAL PART OF THE WORLD — FROM THE DECK OF A SAILING VESSEL.

*Anguilla*

*St. Martin*

*Saba*

*St. Barts*

*Statia*

*St. Kitts*

*Antigua*

*Nevis*

*Mont-serrat*

*Guade-loupe*

*Marie Galante*

*Saintes*

*Dominica*

*Martinique*

*St. Lucia*

*St. Vincent*

*Bequia*

*Grenadines*

*Grenada*

N
W · E
S

# Maverick Sea Fare

### by Dee Carstarphen

*Maverick* IS A SMALL WINDJAMMER THAT TAKES PEOPLE SAILING IN THE CARIBBEAN. PASSENGERS JOIN THE SHIP FOR SCHEDULED CRUISES, AND ENJOY THE BEACHING, SNORKELING AND GOOD SAILING ASSOCIATED WITH THE AREA. MAVERICK CARRIES FOURTEEN PASSENGERS AND, TOGETHER WITH SIX CREW, USUALLY THERE ARE TWENTY ON BOARD.

MAVERICK TRIES TO GIVE FOLKS A TASTE OF THE ISLANDS. WHENEVER POSSIBLE, FRESH FRUITS AND VEGETABLES NATIVE TO THE AREA ARE USED.

SPACE AND REFRIGERATION ARE LIMITED ON A SHIP. OVER THE LAST 15 YEARS, MENUS AND SHIP-BOARD TRICKS TO PLEASE A GUEST'S PALATE HAVE BEEN PERFECTED. THE ORGANILLA RUNS THE SHIP! IT'S A SPANISH HURDY-GURDY WHICH SITS ON A SHELF JUST OFF THE DECK INSIDE THE DOG-HOUSE. IT WAS BUILT IN BARCELONA AND PLAYS 6 SPANISH TUNES WHICH NO ONE CAN QUITE RECOGNIZE. THE COOK PLAYS IT WHEN COFFEE COMES UP IN THE MORNING AND IT AN-NOUNCES EACH MEAL AND TEA TIME THROUGHOUT THE DAY.

1

EARLY MORNINGS ANCHORED OUT IN THE ISLANDS ARE VERY SPECIAL. AWAY FROM ALL CITY NOISES, THERE IS A QUIET PEACEFULNESS. AND, FRESH FROM A MORNING SWIM, THE FIRST CUP OF COFFEE ON DECK IS MAGIC!

BREAKFASTS ARE MOST IMPORTANT ON BOARD. MAVERICKS HAVE A PRETTY ACTIVE DAY, INCLUDING SWIMMING, SNORKELING, EXPLORING AND SAILING. NO CONTINENTAL BREAKFAST WILL DO! THE COOK IS UP BRIGHT AND EARLY TO GET HIS MUFFINS OR BISCUITS IN THE OVEN. MIXES ARE USED AS A GALLEY HELP, AND THANK GOODNESS FOR THEM. SINCE ALL THE MEALS ARE TURNED OUT FROM A SPACE THE SIZE OF AN ORDINARY BROOM CLOSET, THE COOK HAS TO BE A WELL-ORGANIZED GENIUS. EGGS WITH BACON, HAM OR SAUSAGE ARE SERVED EVERY OTHER MORNING. THEY ARE FRIED, SCRAMBLED, BAKED, OMELETS OR FUNNY FONDUE.

## MAVERICK OMELETS

BEAT UP TWO EGGS PER PERSON. ADD 1 TBLSP. WATER FOR EACH EGG AND SALT TO TASTE. SAUTÉ IN A TBLSP. OF BUTTER CHOPPED ONION, CHOPPED GREEN PEPPER, CHOPPED TOMATO, DRAINED MUSHROOMS (OR FRESH, CHOPPED) — ANY OR ALL OF THESE. SET ASIDE. GRATE UP A GOOD PILE OF AMERICAN CHEESE. HEAT A DAB OF BUTTER IN AN OMELET PAN UNTIL IT SIZZLES AND ADD A LADLEFULL OF EGG MIX. ROLL AND SHAKE IT IN THE PAN UNTIL IT JUST SETS AND SLIDE IT OUT LIKE A LARGE CRÊPE ONTO A SERVING PAN. SPRINKLE WITH SOME OF THE VEGETABLES. MAKE ANOTHER OMELET, SLIDE IT OUT ON TOP OF THE FIRST. SPRINKLE WITH SOME CHEESE. REPEAT LAYERS, ALTERNATING VEGETABLES AND CHEESE, UNTIL THERE IS A LAYER FOR EACH PERSON. SPRINKLE THE TOP WITH PARSLEY. TO SERVE, CUT IN WEDGES LIKE A PIE. YOU MAY SERVE UP TO 10 BEFORE THE STACK BECOMES TOO HIGH.

## MAVERICK FUNNY FONDUE

8 SLICES BREAD, BUTTERED     1 tSP. SALT

4 EGGS, BEATEN     1/4 tSP. PEPPER     1 tBLSP. WORCESTERSHIRE

4 C MILK     1/2 LB. SHARP CHEESE, GRATED

BUTTER BAKING DISH AND FIT BREAD IN. ADD MILK, SALT, PEPPER AND WORCESTERSHIRE TO BEATEN EGGS AND MIX. SPRINKLE HALF OF CHEESE ON BREAD. POUR EGG MIX OVER BREAD AND TOP WITH REMAINING CHEESE. LET STAND AT LEAST ONE HOUR. (OVERNITE IS FINE). BAKE AT 350° ONE HOUR. SERVE AS IS OR WITH CREAM OR MUSHROOM SAUCE. SERVES 6-8.

*On* NON-EGG MORNINGS, THERE MAY BE PANCAKES, FRENCH TOAST, HASH OR CREAMED DRIED BEEF ON BISCUITS. SOME FOLKS GROAN AND SAY ~ "OH, *S.O.S.!*", BUT THE SAUCE IS FIXED WITH GREEN PEPPERS, MUSHROOMS AND CHEESE. GUYS WHO HATED IT IN THE SERVICE COME BACK FOR SECONDS. **Hash** IS SEASONED UP WITH ONION, CATSUP AND WORCESTERSHIRE AND BAKED OR FRIED TILL CRUSTY. SOMETIMES HOLES ARE POKED IN THE HASH, EGGS ARE DROPPED IN AND BAKED TILL THEY'RE SET.

*Maverick's* **French Toast** IS SPECIAL. RUM IS SO MUCH A PART OF CARIBBEAN LORE THAT MANY RECIPES HAVE EVOLVED TO UTILIZE ITS LOVELY FLAVOR .... EVEN AT BREAKFAST TIME! YOU MIGHT LIKE TO TRY THIS YOURSELF: PUT 8 SLICES OF BREAD IN A PAN. BEAT 4 EGGS; ADD 1 C EVAPORATED MILK, 2 tBLSP. RUM, 1 tBLSP. SUGAR, 1/4 tSP. SALT, 1/2 tSP. CINNAMON AND 1/4 tSP. NUTMEG. POUR OVER BREAD. TURN TO COAT EVENLY. LET SOAK AT LEAST 1/2 HR. ~ OVERNITE IS O.K. SAUTÉ IN HOT BUTTER UNTIL GOLDEN.

A CHARTER BOAT WE KNOW PUTS 2 SYRUP JUGS ON THE TABLE ~ ONE WITH STRAIGHT SYRUP AND ONE HALF RUM/HALF SYRUP. A JOLLY GOOD WAY TO START THE DAY!

3

$L$UNCHTME IS INFORMAL.

Soup's On

It's SERVED BUFFET-STYLE ON DECK.

$S$OUPS ARE THE MAINSTAY, AND WHATEVER IS LEFT OVER FROM OTHER MEALS MIGHT TURN UP IN THE SOUP POT. SOME OF MAVERICK'S BEST SOUPS ARE MADE FROM LEFT-OVER BEEF STROGANOFF, STEW, CHOP SUEY OR CHICKEN CURRY AND, YES, EVEN SPAGHETTI SOUP HAS MADE ITS APPEARANCE! ALL KINDS OF LIPTONS DRIED SOUPS ARE IN THE CUPBOARD AND ADDED AS FLAVORFULL STOCKS TO LEFTOVERS. LIPTONS PEA SOUP IS ESPECIALLY GOOD IF YOU FRY UP A COUPLE OF CHOPPED ONIONS IN BUTTER — ADD WATER AND SOUP MIX. HEAT UP AS PER PKG. DIREC- TIONS. CHOP UP

2 OR 3 CANS OF VIENNA SAUSAGE (OR A FEW HOT DOGS) FOR THE TOP.

IF THERE'S A HAM BONE, THOUGH, BRING OUT THE DRIED SPLIT PEAS TO MAKE ~

## Dutch Pea Soup

| | | |
|---|---|---|
| LEFT-OVER HAM BONE | ¼ TSP. PEPPER | ¼ TSP. ONION SALT |
| 2⅓ C SPLIT PEAS | ½ BAY LEAF | ¼ TSP. SEASON ALL |
| 2 CARROTS, SLICED THIN | SALT TO TASTE | ¼ TSP. GARLIC SALT |
| 2 ONIONS, CHOPPED | 2 TSP. WORCESTERSHIRE | DASH A-1 SAUCE |
| ¼ TSP. ALLSPICE | ¼ TSP. CELERY SALT | |

IN DUTCH OVEN, HEAT BONE, PEAS, CARROTS, ONIONS AND 7 C WATER TO A BOIL. ADD SEASONINGS; REDUCE HEAT, COVER AND SIMMER 45 MINUTES, OR UNTIL PEAS ARE TENDER. REMOVE ANY MEAT FROM BONE AND RETURN TO SOUP. DISCARD BONE. ADD MORE WATER IF NEEDED AND TASTE FOR SALT. SERVES 10.

SOME DAY, WHEN THE SHIP IS UNDER WAY AT LUNCHTIME, COOKIE WILL FIX HIS **Carribean Beans** AND CORNBREAD. THE BEANS STAY IN THE POT BETTER THAN A SOUP WHEN THE SHIP HEELS OVER.

SAUTÉ THE INEVITABLE CHOPPED ONION, SOME
CHOPPED GREEN PEPPER AND A MINCED CLOVE OR TWO
OF GARLIC IN OIL. ADD ENOUGH QUANTITY OF PORK AND BEANS TO SERVE
THE MOTLEY CREW. ADD A CAN OF CHILI WITHOUT BEANS TO ZIP IT UP AND
ONE OR TWO CANS OF TOMATO SAUCE (8 OZ.). A LITTLE OREGANO TOO, PLEASE!

THESE BEANS ARE SERVED WITH A PAN OF WARM CORNBREAD, FRUIT
AND AN ICE COLD DRINK. A PACKAGED CORNBREAD MIX MAY BE USED.
IF THE MIX IS UNAVAILABLE, HERE'S A GOOD RECIPE:

## MAVERICK CORNBREAD (SERVES 6-8)

| 1 C CORNMEAL | 1/4 C SUGAR | 1 EGG | 3 TSP. BAKING PWD. |
| 1 C FLOUR | 1 TSP. SALT | 1 C MILK | 1/4 C MELTED BUTTER |

COMBINE DRY INGREDIENTS. ADD EGG, MILK AND SHORTENING AND STIR.
POUR INTO GREASED 9" SQUARE PAN AND BAKE AT 425° - 20 MINUTES.

MAVERICK HAS A PICNIC
LUNCH AT A-FAVORITE PLAY SPOT
UP IN THE ISLANDS, AND, IF THE GODS OF
SEA AND WIND ARE KIND, THE SPREAD IS
SET UP IN A ROCKY SHADY CAVE. IT'S A
TYPICAL PICNIC LUNCH WITH SANDWICHES, HARD-
BOILED EGGS, PICKLES, FRUIT AND COOKIES, A
BIG JUG OF COLD JUICE, AND

### (FOR 20) FERNANDO'S MACARONI SALAD

BOIL 1 LARGE BOX OF MACARONI WITH SALT AND 1/4 C FRENCH DRESS-
ING MIXED WITH THE WATER. DRAIN. CHOP 3/4 HEAD CELERY, 1 ONION
AND 2 GREEN PEPPERS. GRATE 4 CARROTS. ADD TO MACARONI WITH 3
CANS DRAINED SHRIMP. SEASON WITH CELERY SALT, ONION SALT, SEA-
SON ALL, AND 1 TSP. CHOPPED PARSLEY. ADD MAYONNAISE TO MOISTEN.
CHOP 4 HARD-BOILED EGGS TO GARNISH. HOORAY FERNANDO!

**Appetites** ARE FIERCE, AFTER PLAYING VOLLEY BALL, CLIMBING ROCKS, SNORKELING AND HIKING!

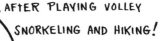

**Sandwich Fillings** ARE PRETTY STANDARD

EGG SALAD IS GOOD WITH A TOUCH OF CURRY PWD., A LITTLE RELISH AND MOIST-ENED WITH MAYONNAISE. SOMETIME TRY TUNA SALAD MIXED WITH CHOPPED CELERY, APPLE AND MAYONNAISE. P-NUT BUTTER AND BACON IS ANOTHER FAVORITE. OPEN-FACED SANDWICHES ARE POPULAR ~ BROILED WITH ANY NUMBER OF COMBINATIONS FROM LUNCHEON MEAT TOPPED WITH CHEESE TO P-NUT BUTTER AND BANANAS. HERE'S:

## FERNANDO'S SEASONED TOAST

FIXED TO HAVE WITH HIS PUMPKIN SOUP OR CONCH CHOWDER (RECIPES FURTHER ON). FOR 30 PIECES OF TOAST: MIX 1½ C MARGARINE (AT ROOM TEMP.), 2 CHOPPED MEDIUM ONIONS, 1 TBLSP. PARSLEY, 1 TBLSP. SESAME SEED, 1 TBLSP. POPPY SEED, ½ TSP. HERB SEASONING (FRENCHS), ½ TSP. SEASON-ALL, ¼ TSP. PEPPER, 1 TSP. WORCESTERSHIRE, AND ⅓ C PARMESAN CHEESE. SPREAD ON BREAD, OVERLAP SLIGHTLY ON BAKING SHEETS AND BAKE AT 400° UNTIL TOASTY.

**By** 4 P.M. ALL HANDS ARE READY FOR A FORTIFIED COFFEE AND TEA. THERE MAY BE COOKIES, COFFEECAKE, BROWNIES OR LEFTOVER MUFFINS AND BISCUITS.

## BROWNIES

HEAT OVEN TO 350°. GREASE AN 8" SQUARE PAN.

| | | |
|---|---|---|
| ¾ C FLOUR | ½ TSP. SALT | 2 EGGS |
| 1 C SUGAR | ½ C BUTTER | 1 TSP. VANILLA |
| 5 TBLSP. UNSWEET COCOA | ½ C CHOPPED NUTS | |

PLACE ALL IN A BOWL. MIX AT MEDIUM SPEED WITH ELECTRIC MIXER UNTIL BLENDED ~ THEN BEAT AT HIGH SPEED 3 MINUTES. POUR IN PAN AND BAKE 30 MINUTES OR UNTIL TOOTHPICK COMES OUT CLEAN. SPRINKLE WITH PWD. SUGAR IF YOU WISH. SERVES 6.

## COFFEECAKE   (FOR 10)

SIFT 2½ C FLOUR, ¾ C SUGAR, ½ tSP. SALT, 1        tSP. NUtMEG.
ADD 1 C BROWN SUGAR. MIX IN ¾ C OIL.              tAKE
AWAY ⅓ OF ABOVE MIX FOR tOPPING. ADD              to
OtHER ⅔, 1 EGG, BEAtEN, 1 C SOUR MILK             (WItH
1 tSP. OF SODA MIXED IN). BLEND
BAttER AND POUR INtO RECtANGULAR
GREASED BAKING PAN. to tOPPING, ADD 1             tSP. CIN-
NAMON AND SPRINKLE OVER CAKE. ADD CHOPPED NUtS IF DESIRED.
BAKE At 350° ~ 45 MINUtES OR UNtIL DONE.

AFtER ANCHORING IN tHE EVENING, WItH SAILS FURLED AND tHE AWNING
SEt, MAVERICK'S BAR OPENS FOR HAPPY HOUR. ~ ~ SUNSEt AND tWI-
LIGHt QUIEt tIME IN A REMOtE COVE WItH tHE WHOLE PANORAMA OF
SEA, SKY AND ISLANDS SPREAD OUt to SHARE. tIME FOR RELAXING,
REVIEWING tHE DAY, GOOD CONVERSAtION WItH SHIPMAtES AND, OF
COURSE, A LIttLE SOMEtHING to SNACK ON WItH YOUR DRINK.

THE LOCKERS HOLD P-NUtS AND ALL KINDS OF CHIPS AND
CURLS AND CRISPS AND PUFFS. IF tHE StOVE ISN'T tOO FULL OF DIN-
NER A-FIXING, SOME CORN MIGHt BE POPPED. A FEW DIPS: ↓↓↓↓↓

1. CottAGE <u>CHEESE</u> MIXED WItH GOOD SEASONS DRESSING MIX
(DRY-ANY FLAVOR) AND A LIttLE MAYONNAISE.

2. <u>CLAM DIP</u> — CREAM 1 - 8 OZ. PKG. CREAM CHEESE WItH 1 CAN
DRAINED MINCED CLAMS. ADD 1 tSP. MINCED ONION, 1 tSP. PARSLEY,
1 tSP. WORCEStERSHIRE, 1 tBLSP. MAYONNAISE, ½ tSP. MUStARD, AND
SALt AND PEPPER to tAStE.

3. UNDERWOODS <u>LIVERWURSt</u>
<u>SPREAD</u> MIXED WItH
A

GRAtING OF RAW ONION AND A tSP. OF BRANDY —
POOR MAN'S PÂtÉ.

CANNED SQUID, CLAMS, OCTO-
PUS, OYSTERS, SARDINES AND THE LIKE
ARE ON HAND, AS WELL AS SEVERAL KINDS
OF CHEESE. OTHER EXOTIC APPETIZER IDEAS ARE
MENTIONED THROUGHOUT THIS BOOK.

## Dinners (BREAKFASTS TOO) ARE ————— SERVED

IN TWO SHIFTS, AS SPACE AT THE TABLE BELOW DECKS IS
LIMITED. THE WATCH THAT EATS FIRST ONE DAY, IS SECOND
THE NEXT. DURING A CRUISE, THERE ARE A COUPLE OF BUFFETS
WHICH MAKE FOR MORE VARIETY AND INFORMALITY FOR ALL. NO
"DRESSING" FOR DINNER ON MAVERICK!

PLENTY OF DRESSING IS ON THE MENU ~ STUFFED IN THE BIRDS!

## Menus VARY ACCORDING                    TO THE AVAILABILITY OF FRESH
PRODUCE. EACH MEAL IS SERVED WITH A FRESH SALAD AND WINE WHEN
APPROPRIATE. THERE ARE ALWAYS DESSERTS AND COFFEE AND TEA
ARE SERVED ON DECK AFTERWARDS. LIQUORS AND BRANDY ARE AVAIL-
ABLE AT THE BAR FOR THOSE WHO WISH THEM. MAVERICK GIVES
HER PEOPLE A FANTASTIC VACATION WITH PLENTY OF GOOD TASTY
FOOD. SOME OF THE MEALS SERVED:

ROAST CHICKEN (TURKEY AT THANKSGIVING AND CHRISTMAS)

| | | |
|---|---|---|
| SWISS STEAK | BAKED HAM | BEEF STROGANOFF |
| WEST INDIAN FISH | CHICKEN CURRY | SHRIMP CREOLE |
| STEW AND DUMPLINGS | MEAT LOAF | LONDON BROIL |
| VEAL PAPRIKA | CHINESE | SPAGHETTI |

8

# SWISS STEAK

SERVES 4

1½ to 2 LB. BONELESS ROUND STEAK. CUT IN SERVING PIECES. MIX ⅓ C FLOUR, 1½ tSP. SALT, ⅛ tSP. PEPPER AND POUND INTO MEAT TILL IT'S TAKEN UP. BROWN MEAT IN 3 TBLSP BACON DRIPPINGS. ADD 1 8-OZ. CAN TOMATO SAUCE, ½ C WATER, 1 tSP. WORCESTERSHIRE AND ½ BAY LEAF (CRUMBLE). COVER AND SIMMER ABOUT ONE HOUR. ADD 2 MEDIUM ONIONS, SLICED, AND 1 GREEN PEPPER, CUT IN RINGS. COVER AND SIMMER 30 MINUTES MORE, OR UNTIL TENDER. SERVE WITH NOODLES OR MASHED POTATOES.

## (SERVES 8) Beef Stew

3½ LB. STEWING BEEF (IN CHUNKS)
3 STRIPS BACON, CHOPPED
1 C SEASONED FLOUR     ½ BAY LEAF
2 CLOVES GARLIC, CRUSHED    ¼ tSP. THYME
2 CANS MUSHROOMS    ¼ tSP. MARJORAM
1 LG. CHOPPED ONION    1 TBLSP. CHOPPED PARSLEY
1 CAN CONSOMMÉ    6 POTATOES, QUARTERED
1 C RED WINE    10 CARROTS, CUT IN CHUNKS
¼ tSP. CLOVES    1 CAN BOILED ONIONS    BISQUICK

FRY UP BACON PIECES AND ADD BEEF WHICH HAS BEEN ROLLED IN SEASONED FLOUR. ADD GARLIC. BROWN MEAT AND ADD MUSHROOMS, CHOPPED ONION, CONSOMMÉ AND WINE. ADD CLOVES, BAY, PARSLEY, MARJORAM AND THYME. COVER AND SIMMER AT LEAST AN HOUR OR UNTIL DONE. STEAM POTATOES AND CARROTS SEPARATELY UNTIL TENDER-CRISP. DRAIN AND MIX WITH MEAT. ADD DRAINED CANNED ONIONS. ADJUST SEASONING. MAKE DUMPLINGS AS PER DIRECTIONS ON BISQUICK BOX. SPRINKLE WITH PARSLEY TO SERVE.

## BAKED HAM WITH FRUIT SAUCE

DRAIN AND HEAT SYRUP FROM 1 CAN EACH SLICED PEACHES AND PINEAPPLE CHUNKS (1 LB. SIZE). MIX 1 TBLSP. CORNSTARCH, 1 TSP. DRY MUSTARD, ¼ TSP. PWD. CLOVES AND 2 TBLSP. VINEGAR. SIMMER WITH SYRUP UNTIL THICK AND CLEAR. STIR IN FRUIT. SLICE A 5-LB. CANNED HAM AND LAYER MEAT IN A BAKING PAN. COVER WITH SAUCE AND BAKE AT 350° FOR ½ HOUR.    FOR 10.

THIS IS A BUOY~ NOT A BOY!

# CHICKEN CURRY

CURRY IS A SHOWY MEAL AND WAS SERVED EVERY CRUISE DURING THE YEARS CAPT. JACK CARSTARPHEN RAN MAVERICK. HE CAME FROM A NAVY FAMILY AND GREW UP EATING CURRY. IT'S SERVED BUFFET-STYLE AND A SHORT-CUT IS USED TO MAKE THE SAUCE....A BEAUTY THING TO FEED A LARGE GROUP WITH A MINIMUM OF EFFORT:

1. UNCLE BENS PLAIN WHITE RICE.
2. SWANSON'S CHICKEN A LA KING (10½ OZ.) ~ 2 CANS FOR 3 PEOPLE. CHICKEN AND GRAVY LEFT OVER FROM ROAST CHICKEN NIGHT ARE ALWAYS ADDED FOR EXTRA MEAT AND FLAVOR.
3. CURRY PWD. TO TASTE.

EACH PERSON IS SERVED RICE AND SAUCE AND A LITTLE FROM EACH "BOY" DISH IS SPRINKLED ON TOP. ~ EVERY BITE IS A COMBINATION OF DIFFERENT TASTES. IN THE FAR EAST, YOU MIGHT RECEIVE YOUR RICE AND SAUCE AT TABLE, AND A BOY WOULD COME AROUND WITH EACH CONDIMENT, HENCE THE SIDE DISHES ARE CALLED ~ __BOYS__

| | | |
|---|---|---|
| 1. CHOPPED BACON | 6. FRENCH FRIED ONION RINGS | 11. CHUTNEY |
| 2. CHOPPED HARD BOILED EGGS | 7. RAISINS | 12. FINE GRIND COFFEE |
| 3. CHOPPED GREEN PEPPER | 8. CHOPPED BANANAS | (JUST A SPRINKLE) |
| 4. TOASTED COCONUT | 9. CHOPPED APPLE OR | 13. CHOPPED PRESERVED |
| 5. CHOPPED P-NUTS | 10. DRAINED CRUSHED PINEAPPLE | GINGER |

IF YOU SERVE ALL OF THESE BOYS, YOU WOULD HAVE A "13 BOY CURRY", AND YOU COULD HAVE MORE OR LESS BOYS ~ CHOPPED TOMATOES, CUCUMBERS OR AVOCADOS ARE NICE, AS IS ORANGE PEEL (CHOPPED VERY FINE), BUT NOT NECESSARY. YOU MAY HAVE AS FEW AS 6, OR AS MANY AS 20, DEPENDING ON HOW FANCY YOU WANT TO BE.

# 拓 Chinese Beef 本 FEEDS 8

HEAT ¼ C OIL UNTIL SMOKING. SEAR 1-1½ LB. MINUTE STEAK OR SIRLOIN, CUT IN THIN STRIPS. STIR IN 1 C COARSE-CHOPPED GREEN PEPPER, 1 C COARSE-CHOPPED ONIONS AND 2 C COARSE-CHOPPED CELERY. STIR-FRY A COUPLE OF MINUTES. ADD DRAINED MUSHROOMS, PEA PODS (PLUS ANY ORIENTAL VEGETABLES — WATER CHESTNUTS, BAMBOO SHOOTS, BEAN SPROUTS OR FANCY CHINESE VEGETABLES). ADD 1 CAN CONSOMMÉ. MIX 2 TBLSP. CORNSTARCH WITH 1½ TBLSP. HEINZ BROWNING, 1 TBLSP. SOY, 1 TSP. RAW SUGAR AND ENOUGH WATER TO MAKE A SMOOTH PASTE. ADD TO MEAT AND VEGETABLES AND STIR UNTIL THICK. DO NOT OVERCOOK! SERVE OVER RICE..... PLACE CHINESE NOODLES AND SWEET AND SOUR SAUCE ON THE TABLE.

Maverick SPAGHETTI SAUCE IS MADE A COUPLE OF DIFFERENT WAYS. SINCE THE SHIP IS SAILING EVERY DAY, IT'S DIFFICULT TO SIMMER A LARGE POT OF SAUCE ON THE STOVE FOR HOURS, SO THE COOK CHEATS A LITTLE. EITHER FRENCH'S SPAGHETTI SAUCE MIX IS USED, ADDING PLENTY OF HAMBURGER TO BEEF IT UP, OR THIS SAUCE IS MADE: SAUTÉ 1 CHOPPED ONION, 1 MINCED CLOVE GARLIC AND ½ TSP. OREGANO IN OIL UNTIL SOFT. ADD 2 CANS (1 LB.) CHILI WITHOUT BEANS AND 1 CAN (8 OZ) TOMATO SAUCE. SIMMER A FEW MINUTES AND SERVE OVER SPAGHETTI. ON THE TABLE — PARMESAN, GREEN SALAD, RED WINE AND HOT GARLIC BREAD. SERVES 5 OR 6

Here's A RECIPE FOR FRENCH BREAD SERVED WITH SPAGHETTI. EVEN IF YOU DON'T HAVE STEAM IN YOUR OVEN AND TILES TO BAKE THE LOAVES ON LIKE IN THE OLD COUNTRY, THEY'RE CRUSTY AND BROWN ON THE OUTSIDE ~ TENDER AND NOT TOO FINE-GRAINED ON THE INSIDE. SLASH IT DIAGONALLY, SLOP IT WITH GARLIC BUTTER AND RE-HEAT IT. — DELICIOUS! A LOAF TO BE PROUD OF ——→ —→ —→ ↗

11

# MAVERICK French Bread

SPRINKLE 1 PKG. DRY YEAST ON 1/4 C LUKE-WARM WATER IN A SMALL BOWL. LET STAND 5 MINUTES AND STIR UNTIL DISSOLVED. POUR 1 C BOILING WATER OVER 1 TBLSP. BUTTER, 2 TSP. SALT AND 1 TBLSP. SUGAR IN A LARGE BOWL. ADD 3/4 C COLD WATER, STIR AND LET COOL UNTIL LUKEWARM. STIR IN YEAST. GRADUALLY BEAT IN ENOUGH FLOUR TO FORM A STIFF DOUGH (6 C MORE OR LESS). TURN OUT ON A FLOURED BOARD AND KNEAD UNTIL SMOOTH AND SATINY, ADDING MORE FLOUR IF NECESSARY. DUMP IN A LARGE GREASED BOWL, OIL THE TOP, COVER WITH A TOWEL AND LET RISE UNTIL DOUBLE IN BULK. BEAT DOWN AND SHAPE INTO TWO OBLONG LOAVES ABOUT 14" LONG. PLACE ON GREASED BAKING SHEET AND LET RISE UNTIL DOUBLE. BEAT 1 EGG WHITE FROTHY AND BRUSH THE TOPS OF THE LOAVES. WITH A RAZOR, MAKE 3 SLASHES ACROSS TOPS. BAKE AT 425° – 30 MINUTES. REDUCE HEAT TO 350° AND BAKE 20 MINUTES MORE OR UNTIL WELL-BROWNED. BREAK BREAD AWAY FROM PANS TO COOL.

FOR ANYONE WHO LIKES TO BAKE BREAD, YOU MIGHT LIKE TO TRY SOME OF THE FOLLOWING ~ MOSTLY DISCOVERED IN PAST YEARS CRUISING AND LIVING ON SMALLER SAILBOATS THAN MAVERICK.

## A QUICK AND EASY BATTER BREAD ~~ NO-KNEAD WHITE BREAD

| | |
|---|---|
| 1 1/4 C WARM WATER | 2 TSP. SALT |
| 1 PKG. DRY YEAST | 2 TSP. SUGAR |
| 2 TBLSP. SHORTENING | 3 C FLOUR |

DISSOLVE YEAST IN WATER. ADD SHORTENING, SALT, SUGAR AND HALF OF FLOUR. BEAT 300 STROKES OR 2 MINUTES AT MEDIUM SPEED ON MIXER. ADD REST OF FLOUR AND BLEND UNTIL SMOOTH. LET RISE ABOUT 30 MINUTES. BEAT 25 STROKES AND SPREAD IN A GREASED BREAD PAN. LET RISE 40 MINUTES AND BAKE AT 375° UNTIL BROWN AND DONE. MAKES 1 LOAF. YOU MAY THROW IN A HANDFULL OF WHEAT GERM, CRACKED WHEAT, FLAX SEED, SESAME SEED, OR WHATEVER !

FLOUR

12

# CHEESE-CARAWAY BREAD

| | | |
|---|---|---|
| 2 PKG. DRY YEAST | 6½ C FLOUR | |
| 1½ C WARM WATER | 2 EGGS, BEATEN | |
| 2 TBLSP. SUGAR | 2 C GRATED AMERICAN CHEESE | |
| 2¼ TSP. SALT | ¼ C CARAWAY SEEDS | MELTED BUTTER |

SPRINKLE YEAST ON WATER. STIR IN SUGAR AND SALT UNTIL DISSOLVED. ADD 2
C FLOUR AND BEAT WELL. ADD EGGS, CHEESE AND SEEDS AND BEAT. BEAT
IN 4 C FLOUR AND TURN OUT ON A FLOURED BOARD. LET DOUGH REST 10 MINUTES,
KNEAD UNTIL SMOOTH, ADDING MORE FLOUR IF NECESSARY. PLACE IN GREASED
BOWL, OIL TOP AND LET RISE UNTIL DOUBLE. PUNCH DOWN AND LET REST 10
MINUTES AGAIN. SHAPE INTO 2 LOAVES AND PUT IN
GREASED BREAD PANS. LET RISE UNTIL DOUBLE AND
BAKE AT 350° UNTIL GOOD TOASTED!
DONE.

## OATMEAL BREAD

| | | |
|---|---|---|
| 1 C ROLLED OATS | 2 PKG. DRY YEAST | |
| ½ C MOLASSES | JUICE 1 ORANGE PLUS WATER TO MAKE 1-¾ C LIQUID | |
| ¼ C SHORTENING | ½ C WARM WATER | |
| 1 TBLSP. SALT | 6 C FLOUR | 2 TBLSP. SHORTENING |

PUT OATS, MOLASSES, SHORTENING, AND SALT IN BOWL. HEAT JUICE AND
WATER TO A BOIL AND ADD TO OATS; LET STAND TILL MIXTURE IS LUKEWARM.
DISSOLVE YEAST IN ½ C WARM WATER AND STIR INTO OATS. ADD FLOUR.
STIR AND TURN OUT ON A FLOURED BOARD AND KNEAD UNTIL SMOOTH. PUT
IN A GREASED BOWL, OIL THE TOP, COVER AND LET RISE UNTIL DOUBLE.
PUNCH DOWN AND FORM INTO 2 LOAVES. PLACE IN GREASED BREAD
PANS. LET RISE UNTIL DOUBLE AND BAKE AT 350° TILL BROWN AND DONE.

# ONION BREAD

SOFTEN 2 PKG. DRY YEAST IN ½ C WARM WATER. MIX 2 TBLSP. SHORTENING WITH 1½ C HOT WATER UNTIL MELTED.

STIR IN 3 TBLSP. SUGAR, 2 TSP. SALT, AND 1 PKG. LIPTONS DRY ONION SOUP. WHEN LUKEWARM, ADD YEAST MIX. ADD 5½-6 C FLOUR — TURN OUT ON FLOURED BOARD AND KNEAD UNTIL SMOOTH. PUT IN GREASED BOWL, OIL THE TOP, COVER AND LET RISE TILL DOUBLE. PUNCH DOWN AND FORM INTO 2 LOAVES. PLACE IN GREASED BREAD PANS AND LET RISE. BAKE AT 375° UNTIL DONE.

FOR A SPECIAL TIME, EASTER OR CHRISTMAS, MAKE BRIOCHES. YOU CAN MIX UP THE DOUGH THE NIGHT BEFORE, REFRIGERATE IT AND PROCEED THE NEXT MORNING.

## Guadeloupe Brioches

| | | |
|---|---|---|
| ¾ C MILK | ½ C BUTTER | 2 C FLOUR |
| 1 PKG. DRY YEAST | 2½ C FLOUR | ¾ TSP. LEMON EXT. |
| ¼ C WARM WATER | ½ C SUGAR | 1 TSP. GRATED LIME |
| 1 TSP. SUGAR | 3 EGGS, BEATEN | OR LEMON RIND |

SCALD MILK. COOL. SPRINKLE YEAST ON WARM WATER. ADD TSP. OF SUGAR AND LET DISSOLVE. BEAT BUTTER UNTIL SOFT WITH SUGAR. POUR IN MILK, YEAST, EGGS, 2 C FLOUR, FLAVORING, RIND; BEAT UNTIL BLENDED. ADD REST OF FLOUR, TURN OUT ON A FLOURED BOARD AND KNEAD TILL SMOOTH. PLACE IN LARGE BOWL, BRUSH WITH OIL, COVER AND REFRIGERATE OVER NIGHT. DIVIDE DOUGH IN HALF. ROLL EACH HALF TO 14 X 6". CUT 16-18 STRIPS AND TIE EACH STRIP IN A SIMPLE KNOT. PLACE ON GREASED BAKING SHEETS, LET RISE AND BAKE AT 375° UNTIL LIGHTLY BROWNED. GLAZE WHILE WARM WITH 1¼ C CONFECTIONERS SUGAR, 2 TBLSP. WARM WATER AND ¼ TSP. LEMON EXTRACT.     MAKES 36.

14

# 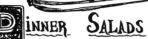INNER SALADS

SALADS SERVED WITH DINNER
ARE VARIED IN SEVERAL WAYS.
TO THE BASIC GREENS ARE ADDED
CUCUMBERS, GREEN PEPPERS, CELERY, TOMATOES, OR
CARROTS. DRESSINGS ARE MADE FROM GOOD SEASONS
PKG. MIXES.... ANY OF THEIR SEVERAL KINDS —
SOMETIMES MIXED.

FOR A CHANGE, THERE MAY BE FRUIT SALAD WITH FRESH
OR CANNED FRUITS, THE DRESSING A MIXTURE OF MAYONNAISE
AND SOUR CREAM (TRY ADDING A TOUCH OF CINNAMON), OR SOME
COTTAGE OR CREAM CHEESE MASHED IN, THINNED WITH A BIT OF
FRUIT JUICE OR LIME. CANNED MANDARIN ORANGES ARE A
TREAT AND SOMETIME ADD CHOPPED PRESERVED GINGER TO SPICE
THINGS UP. TO COLE SLAW, ADD A FEW RAISINS, A TSP. OF SUGAR
AND A DAB OF HOT MUSTARD. ANOTHER FAVORITE IS GRATED CABBAGE
MIXED WITH DRAINED CRUSHED PINEAPPLE AND MARSHMALLOW
BITS MOISTENED WITH MAYONNAISE AND/OR SOUR CREAM....
ADD A FEW CHERRIES FOR COLOR.

IF FRESH SUPPLIES RUN SHORT, A VEGETABLE SALAD
MAY BE MADE. THIS HAS BEEN SERVED AT LUNCHTIME. USE WHAT-
EVER RAW VEGETABLES ARE LEFT PLUS CANNED KIDNEY BEANS,
GREEN BEANS, WATER CHESTNUTS, ARTICHOKE HEARTS, EVEN
BEAN SPROUTS (ALL WELL-DRAINED) ~ WHATEVER SOUNDS
GOOD TO YOU, WITH THE FOLLOWING DRESSING : RUB
THE BOWL WITH GARLIC. MIX TOGETHER 5 TBLSP. VINEGAR, 2
TBLSP. SUGAR, 1/2 TSP. SALT, 1 TSP. PAPRIKA, 1/2 TSP. MUSTARD, 1 TSP.
OREGANO, 1 SLICED ONION AND 4 TBLSP. OIL.

15

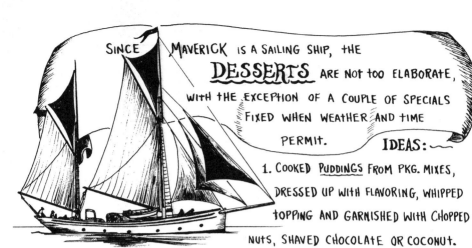

SINCE MAVERICK IS A SAILING SHIP, THE DESSERTS ARE NOT TOO ELABORATE, WITH THE EXCEPTION OF A COUPLE OF SPECIALS FIXED WHEN WEATHER AND TIME PERMIT. IDEAS:

1. COOKED PUDDINGS FROM PKG. MIXES, DRESSED UP WITH FLAVORING, WHIPPED TOPPING AND GARNISHED WITH CHOPPED NUTS, SHAVED CHOCOLATE OR COCONUT.

2. COMSTOCK PIE FILLINGS ARE USED AND CAKE MIXES KEPT ON HAND IN CASE OF AN UNEXPECTED BIRTHDAY.

3. GINGERBREAD IS MIXED UP AND POURED OVER MELTED BUTTER, BROWN SUGAR AND FRUIT, BAKED AND SERVED WITH WHIPPED TOPPING.

4. HOW ABOUT A COBBLER, USING COMSTOCK (ANY FRUIT) PIE FILLING (MIX DIFFERENT KINDS TOGETHER—EVEN MINCEMEAT)...TOPPING MADE WITH BISQUICK SHORT-CAKE DOUGH, SUGAR AND CINNAMON SPRINKLED OVER AND BAKED TILL BROWN AND BUBBLY. YOU MIGHT THROW SOME CHOPPED NUTS ON TOP.

5. FRESH FRUIT CUP ~ LAYERS OF PINEAPPLE, ORANGE, BANANA, PAPAYA, MANGO - EACH LAYER SPRINKLED WITH SHREDDED COCONUT AND RAW SUGAR. TOP EACH SERVING WITH A SPOONFUL OF COCONUT CREAM (SEE INFO ON COCONUT). CANNED PEACHES ARE ACCEPTABLE CHILLED AND SERVED WITH A TBLSP. OF COINTREAU OVER EACH PORTION.

6. APPLE SNOW — CHILL APPLESAUCE AND SHORTLY BEFORE SERVING, BEAT A COUPLE OF EGG WHITES STIFF WITH 2 TBLSP. SUGAR (5 WHITES FOR 20) AND FOLD INTO APPLESAUCE ALONG WITH A LITTLE CRÈME DE MENTHE. THAT'S NICE AND COOLING AFTER CURRY OR SPAGHETTI.

7. PEAR BUCKLE ~ MIX 2 C BISQUICK WITH 2 TBLSP. SUGAR. CUT IN ¼ C BUTTER AND PRESS OVER BOTTOM AND SIDES OF A SQ. BAKING PAN. DRAIN PEARS AND PLACE 6-9 HALVES CUT SIDE DOWN IN ROWS ON PASTRY; SPRINKLE WITH ⅓ C SUGAR. BAKE AT 375° — 15 MINUTES. POUR OVER PEARS A MIX OF 2 BEATEN EGG YOLKS AND 1 C SOUR CREAM. SPRINKLE WITH NUTMEG AND ¼ C SLIVERED ALMONDS. BAKE 30 MINUTES TILL SET. SERVE WARM TO 9.

8. QUICK LEMON-CHEESE PIE ~ HEAT A CAN OF COMSTOCK LEMON PIE FILLING AND BEAT IN 8 OZ. CREAM CHEESE. COOL AND POUR INTO A GRAHAM CRUST. SERVE TOPPED WITH SOUR CREAM. IF THERE'S TIME TO MAKE THE REAL THING, THE FOLLOWING RECIPE IS DELICIOUS ~ LIFTED FROM A DANISH FRIEND.

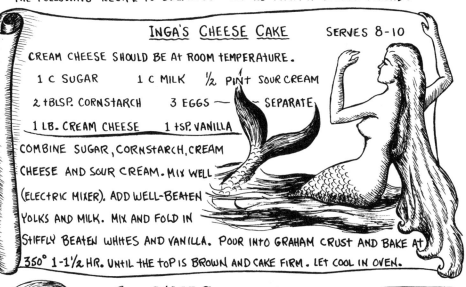

## INGA'S CHEESE CAKE          SERVES 8-10

CREAM CHEESE SHOULD BE AT ROOM TEMPERATURE.

1 C SUGAR      1 C MILK    ½ PINT SOUR CREAM

2 TBLSP. CORNSTARCH      3 EGGS ——— SEPARATE

1 LB. CREAM CHEESE      1 TSP. VANILLA

COMBINE SUGAR, CORNSTARCH, CREAM CHEESE AND SOUR CREAM. MIX WELL (ELECTRIC MIXER). ADD WELL-BEATEN YOLKS AND MILK. MIX AND FOLD IN STIFFLY BEATEN WHITES AND VANILLA. POUR INTO GRAHAM CRUST AND BAKE AT 350° 1-1½ HR. UNTIL THE TOP IS BROWN AND CAKE FIRM. LET COOL IN OVEN.

# CAKES

## BOOZE CAKE

IN SAUCEPAN, BOIL 3 C RAISINS AND 3 C WATER 15 MINUTES. COOL. ADD: —

| | | | |
|---|---|---|---|
| 1 C OIL | 3 EGGS | 3 C FLOUR | 2 TSP. ALLSPICE |
| 1 C BROWN SUGAR | | 2 TSP. BAKING SODA | 1 TSP. CLOVES |
| 1 C WHITE SUGAR | | 2 TSP. CINNAMON | 1 C CHOPPED NUTS |

MIX ALL TOGETHER THOROUGHLY AND BAKE IN LARGE OBLONG GREASED BAKING PAN AT 375° ABOUT 1 HR. OR UNTIL DONE. MAKES 1 LARGE LOAF. KEEPS WELL.

## MAYONNAISE CAKE

| #1 | #2 | #3 |
|---|---|---|
| 1 C RAISINS | 2 EGGS | 3 C FLOUR |
| 1 C NUTMEATS | 1 C SALAD OIL | 2 C SUGAR |
| 2 C BOILING WATER | ½ TSP. SALT | 1½ TSP. MIXED SPICES |
| 2 TSP. SODA | | 6 TBLSP. UNSWEET COCOA |

#1: MIX AND COOL

#2: BEAT TOGETHER LIKE MAYONNAISE

MIX PART 2 AND 3. ADD PART 1. BAKE IN LARGE GREASED OBLONG PAN 40 MINUTES AT 325° OR UNTIL DONE.

## GROUND ORANGE CAKE

GRIND TOGETHER 1 ORANGE, PULP AND RIND (SAVE JUICE), 1 C RAISINS, 1/3 C NUTS. SIFT 2 C FLOUR, 1 TSP. SODA, 1 TSP. SALT, 1 C SUGAR. ADD 1/2 C SHORTENING AND 3/4 C MILK. BEAT 300 STROKES. ADD 2 EGGS, AND 1/4 C MILK. BEAT 300 STROKES. FOLD IN ORANGE- RAISIN MIX. POUR IN GREASED OBLONG BAKING PAN AND BAKE AT 350° FOR 40-50 MINUTES. TOPPING: DRIP 1/3 C ORANGE JUICE OVER WARM CAKE. COMBINE 1/3 C SUGAR, 1 TSP. CINNAMON, 1/4 C CHOPPED NUTS AND SPRINKLE OVER CAKE.

## ORANGE RUM CAKE

| | | |
|---|---|---|
| GRATED RINDS 2 ORANGES AND 2 LIMES | | |
| JUICE OF 2 ORANGES AND 2 LIMES | | 1/2 TSP. SALT |
| 1 C BUTTER | 2 1/2 C FLOUR | 1 C BUTTERMILK |
| 2 C SUGAR | 1 TSP. BAKING SODA | 1 C CHOPPED NUTS |
| 2 EGGS | 2 TSP. BAKING PWD. | 2 TBLSP. RUM |

PREPARE RINDS AND JUICES. BEAT BUTTER WITH 1 C SUGAR. ADD RINDS AND EGGS. SIFT FLOUR, SODA, BAKING PWD. AND SALT. ADD ALTERNATELY WITH MILK. FOLD IN NUTS. BAKE IN GREASED TUBE PAN AT 350° 1 HOUR OR TILL DONE. MEAN- WHILE, STRAIN JUICE. ADD 1 C SUGAR AND RUM. BRING TO A BOIL AND POUR SLOWLY OVER WARM CAKE. LET STAND A DAY OR TWO FOR BEST EATING.

## FROSTED COFFEE BARS

| | | |
|---|---|---|
| 2 TSP. INSTANT COFFEE | 1 C BROWN SUGAR | 1/2 TSP. CINNAMON |
| 1/2 C HOT WATER | 1 EGG | 1/2 C CHOPPED NUTS |
| 1/2 C BUTTER | 1 1/2 C FLOUR | 1/2 C RAISINS |
| | 1/2 TSP. SODA | 1 C PWD. SUGAR |
| | 1/8 TSP. SALT | 3 TBLSP. CREAM |
| | 1/2 TSP. BAKING PWD. | 1/2 TSP. VANILLA |

DISSOLVE COFFEE IN WATER. COOL. CREAM BUTTER AND SUGAR; ADD EGG. BEAT IN WARM COFFEE. SIFT DRY INGREDIENTS AND ADD. STIR IN NUTS AND RAISINS. SPREAD IN A GREASED 10 X 15" BAKING PAN. BAKE AT 350°– 15 MINUTES. MIX PWD. SUGAR, CREAM AND VANILLA. FROST BARS WHILE WARM. SERVES 8.

# GRASSHOPPER PIE

26 MARSHMALLOWS     ½ C MILK

3 tBLSP. GREEN CRÈME DE MENTHE

3 tBLSP CRÈME DE CACAO

1 C CREAM, WHIPPED

PUT MARSHMALLOWS IN A DOUBLE BOILER.
ADD MILK AND HEAT TILL JUST MELTED. COOL. FOLD
LIQUORS INTO CREAM. FOLD IN MARSHMALLOW MIXTURE.
POUR INTO PIE SHELL AND CHILL. GARNISH WITH WHIPPED CREAM AND CHOCOLATE
SHAVINGS. CRUST MAY BE MADE FROM 18 CHOCOLATE COOKIES, CRUSHED, MIXED
WITH WITH ½ C BUTTER AND PRESSED INTO A 9" PIE PAN. IF YOU WISH, SERVE
MINUS CRUST IN DESSERT CUPS.

It's NICE WHEN DESSERTS ARE ASSOCIATED WITH THE CARIBBEAN, BUT MAVER-
ICK ISN'T IMMUNE TO BORROWING WHEN THE RESULTS ARE AS FINE AS :—

## JoAnne WEETER'S DERBY PIE (KENTUCKY, OF COURSE)

| | | |
|---|---|---|
| ¼ C BUTTER | ¼ tSP. SALT | 2 tBLSP. KENTUCKY BOURBON |
| 1 C SUGAR | 1 tSP. VANILLA | 1 - 9" UNBAKED PIE SHELL |
| 3 EGGS | ½ C CHOCOLATE CHIPS | |
| ¾ C LITE CORN SYRUP | ½ C CHOPPED BLACK WALNUTS | |

CREAM BUTTER AND ADD SUGAR GRADUALLY. ADD BEATEN EGGS, SYRUP, SALT
AND VANILLA. ADD CHOCOLATE CHIPS, NUTS AND BOURBON AND STIR WELL.
POUR INTO CRUST AND BAKE AT 375° — 40-50 MINUTES. GOOD COLD OR WARM.
MAY BE GARNISHED WITH WHIPPED CREAM. IT'S PRETTY RICH, SO 1 PIE WILL
SERVE 9 OR 10.

LIQUOR IS STILL ONE OF THE BIG BARGAINS LEFT IN THE WEST INDIES. PERHAPS
THAT'S WHY A LOT OF THE DESSERTS HAVE BOOZE IN THEM. CONSEQUENTLY, THE
END OF THIS DESSERT LIST SHOULD MENTION TWO MORE VERY NICE WAYS TO
FINISH A MEAL:

     1. WITH IRISH COFFEE (CARIBBEAN COFFEE IF MADE WITH RUM)

OR— 2. A PLATE OF FRESH FRUIT, CHEESE AND A WEE NIP OF BRANDY.

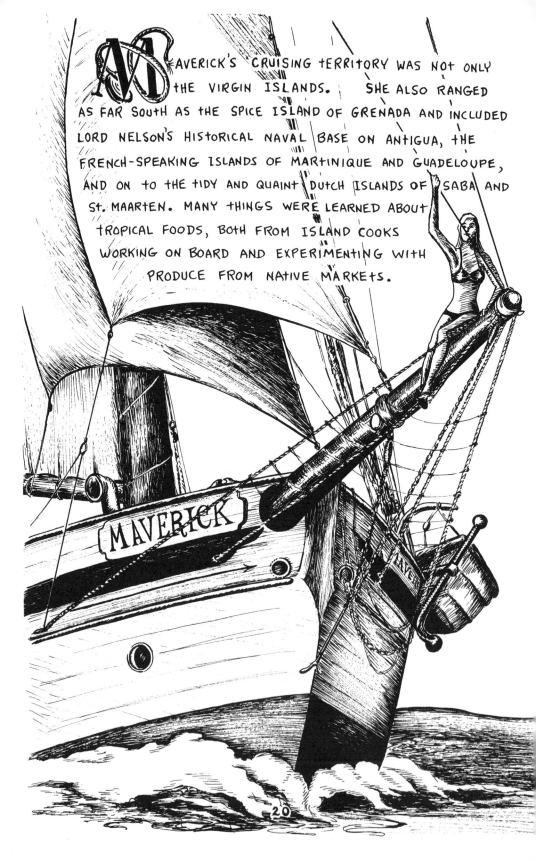

MAVERICK'S CRUISING TERRITORY WAS NOT ONLY THE VIRGIN ISLANDS. SHE ALSO RANGED AS FAR SOUTH AS THE SPICE ISLAND OF GRENADA AND INCLUDED LORD NELSON'S HISTORICAL NAVAL BASE ON ANTIGUA, THE FRENCH-SPEAKING ISLANDS OF MARTINIQUE AND GUADELOUPE, AND ON TO THE TIDY AND QUAINT DUTCH ISLANDS OF SABA AND St. MAARTEN. MANY THINGS WERE LEARNED ABOUT TROPICAL FOODS, BOTH FROM ISLAND COOKS WORKING ON BOARD AND EXPERIMENTING WITH PRODUCE FROM NATIVE MARKETS.

MAVERICK

*the* **Coconut** IS THE MOST
VERSATILE OF ALL TROPICAL
FRUITS. WHEN YOUNG AND
GREEN, THE COCONUT MAY BE
TAPPED AND USED AS A REFRESH-
ING DRINK. THE MEAT IS STILL
A JELLY AT THIS STAGE AND MOST OF THE FLAVOR
IS IN THE WATER. THE JELLY IS SOMETIMES FED TO
BABIES. AS THE NUT MATURES, THE COCONUT WATER
DECREASES AND THE FLAVOR GOES INTO DE-
VELOPING THE NUT. WHEN RIPE, THE MEAT IS
SWEETER. AS THE NUT BECOMES OLDER STILL,
IT DRIES UP AND BECOMES MORE OILY. IN THE
PACIFIC, THE MEAT OF THE OLDER NUTS IS
LEFT OUT IN THE SUN TO DRY AND THEN SOLD AS
COPRA FOR THE OIL — ONE OF THE PUREST TO BE FOUND
ANYWHERE. THERE ARE WAYS TO HELP YOU MORE EASILY
REMOVE THE COCONUT MEAT FROM THE SHELL. REMOVE THE
WATER FIRST BY POKING HOLES IN THE EYES WITH AN ICE PICK AND
POURING IT OFF.        THEN EITHER:

1. TAP WELL ALL OVER WITH A HAMMER BEFORE CRACKING.
OR
2. BAKE IN A 350° OVEN FOR 20 MINUTES BEFORE CRACKING.
HIT SHARPLY WITH A HAMMER ALL AROUND THE MIDDLE TILL SHE CRACKS.
POP MEAT OUT WITH A BLUNT KNIFE.

WHEN THE ISLANDERS TALK ABOUT USING THE COCONUT MILK OR
CREAM, THEY'RE NOT TALKING ABOUT THE WATER FOUND INSIDE
THE NUT. OH NO! — IT'S NOT AS EASY AS THAT! YOU MUST
GRATE THE COCONUT FINELY AND THEN PRESS OR SQUEEZE
THE GRATINGS IN CHEESECLOTH. THE DRIPPINGS ARE A
RICH CREAM WHICH MAY BE USED ON DESSERTS OR IN
COFFEE AS REGULAR CREAM. COCONUT MILK

...IS MADE BY SOAKING THE GRATINGS IN MILK OR WATER FOR 15 MINUTES, HEATING IT AND THEN SQUEEZING THE WHOLE BUNCH THROUGH CHEESECLOTH. THIS IS STILL DONE IN THE ISLANDS AS IT WAS 100 YEARS AGO. ON MAVERICK IT WAS FOUND EASIER TO USE THE FINE BLADE OF THE MEAT GRINDER (CATCHING ALL THE JUICE THAT DRIPS OUT) AND THEN SQUEEZING THE GRINDS. IF YOU HAVE A BLENDER, YOU MAY MAKE IT THE SIMPLEST WAY OF ALL BY PUTTING SMALL CHUNKS IN YOUR BLENDER AND WHIRRING IT TILL YOU HAVE A THICK SMOOTH CREAM.

THERE IS ALSO A CANNED PRODUCT MADE IN PUERTO RICO THAT WILL DO NICELY IN A PINCH — CALLED "CREAM OF COCONUT" AND PUT OUT BY GOYA OR LOPEZ, IT'S NOT AS GOOD AS THE FRESH, BUT MAY BE SUBSTITUTED IN MANY RECIPES.

## Coconut Chips (AN APPETIZER)

GRATE FRESH COCONUT WITH A VEGETABLE PEELER, SALT LAYERS IN A WOODEN BOWL AND LET SIT AN HOUR OR TWO BEFORE SERVING....OR SPREAD THE CHIPS OUT ON A COOKIE SHEET AND TOAST IN A 375° OVEN UNTIL THE EDGES ARE NICELY BROWNED. SALT THESE TOO!

## Coconut Spoon Bread

| | | |
|---|---|---|
| 3 ½ C MILK | 1 ½ tSP. SALT | 3 EGGS |
| 1 C CORNMEAL | 2 tBLSP. BUTTER | ½ C COCONUT CREAM |

HEAT 3 C MILK. MIX REMAINING MILK AND COCONUT CREAM WITH CORNMEAL. ADD CORNMEAL MIX TO MILK AND COOK UNTIL THICK, STIRRING. ADD SALT. REMOVE FROM HEAT AND ADD BUTTER AND BEATEN EGGS. MIX WELL. POUR INTO 1 ½ QT. BAKING DISH AND BAKE AT 425° — 45 MINUTES. SERVE WARM. TRY WITH FISH. SERVES 6.

# E.J.'s WEST INDIAN COCONUT BREAD

GRATE 1 COCONUT, ANY SIZE AND ADD:

| | | |
|---|---|---|
| ½ tsp. CINNAMON | 2 tBLSP. SOFT BUTTER | 2 tSP. BAKING PWD. |
| ½ tsp. NUTMEG | ¼ c COCONUT WATER | 2 EGGS, BEATEN |
| ½ tsp. SALT | ½ c MILK | 1 tSP. VANILLA |
| 2 c FLOUR | ¾ – 1 c SUGAR (DEPENDING ON TASTE) | |

STIR ALL IN A BOWL UNTIL PROPERLY DISSOLVED TO A THICK PASTE. IF DE-
SIRED TO MAKE IT FESTIVE, YOU MAY ADD UP TO A CUP OF MIXED PEEL,
RAISINS OR CHERRIES. POUR INTO A 9 X 5" GREASED BREAD PAN
AND BAKE AT 350° AN HOUR OR TILL DONE. SERVE WARM.

## Coconut Rice

| | |
|---|---|
| 2 MEDIUM ONIONS, CHOPPED | 1 C COCONUT CREAM |
| 2 tBLSP. OIL | ¼ C PRESERVED GINGER, SLICED |
| 2 C RICE | 3 C CHICKEN BROTH |
| 1 CAN WATER CHESTNUTS (8 OZ.) | SALT AND PEPPER |

FRY ONIONS IN OIL UNTIL SOFT. ADD RICE AND STIR-FRY UNTIL
GOLDEN. ADD WATER CHESTNUTS (SLICED) AND GINGER. ADD
COCONUT CREAM AND CHICKEN BROTH. SALT AND PEPPER TO
TASTE. COVER AND SIMMER 20 MIN. UNTIL LIQUID'S ABSORBED.

## Coconut Soufflé    SERVES 6

| | |
|---|---|
| 1 tBLSP. UNFLAVORED GELATIN | 1 C COCONUT CREAM |
| 4 EGGS, SEPARATED | 1 C FINE GRATED FRESH COCONUT |
| ¼ C SUGAR | GRATED RIND 1 LIME |

SOFTEN GELATIN IN ¼ C COLD WATER. HEAT UNTIL DISSOLVED.
SET ASIDE. BEAT YOLKS WELL WITH SUGAR TILL LIGHT AND FORM A
RIBBON. PUT IN DOUBLE BOILER OVER HOT WATER AND
POUR IN COCONUT CREAM, BEATING. COOK OVER LOW
HEAT, STIRRING, TILL CUSTARD IS THICK ENOUGH
TO COAT SPOON. REMOVE FROM HEAT AND STIR
IN GRATED COCONUT, LIME RIND AND GELATIN.
CHILL UNTIL MIXTURE MOUNDS. BEAT WHITES STIFF
AND FOLD INTO CUSTARD. REFRIGERATE UNTIL FIRM.

23

# Bananas

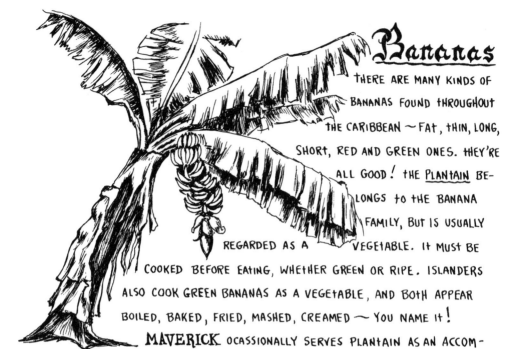

THERE ARE MANY KINDS OF BANANAS FOUND THROUGHOUT THE CARIBBEAN — FAT, THIN, LONG, SHORT, RED AND GREEN ONES. THEY'RE ALL GOOD! THE <u>PLANTAIN</u> BELONGS TO THE BANANA FAMILY, BUT IS USUALLY REGARDED AS A VEGETABLE. IT MUST BE COOKED BEFORE EATING, WHETHER GREEN OR RIPE. ISLANDERS ALSO COOK GREEN BANANAS AS A VEGETABLE, AND BOTH APPEAR BOILED, BAKED, FRIED, MASHED, CREAMED — YOU NAME IT!

MAVERICK OCASSIONALLY SERVES PLANTAIN AS AN ACCOMPANIMENT TO FISH OR MEAT. THE SKINS ARE BLACK WHEN RIPE. THEY'RE PEELED, SLICED AND ROLLED IN FLOUR THAT'S HAD EITHER A LITTLE CURRY PWD. OR CINNAMON ADDED; SAUTÉED IN BUTTER UNTIL GOLDEN.

## <u>PLANTAIN SNACKS</u> :

1. DIP RIPE CHUNKS OF PLANTAIN IN A BISQUICK BATTER AND DEEP FRY TILL GOLDEN BROWN.

2. THINLY SLICE GREEN PLANTAIN CHIPS AND DEEP FRY UNTIL CRISP AND BROWN. DRAIN ON PAPER TOWEL. SPRINKLE WITH SALT.

AN EASY DINNER — <u>HAM-BANANA ROLLS</u> : SPREAD THIN SLICES OF HAM WITH A STRIPE OF P-NUT BUTTER AND A SWIPE OF MUSTARD. WRAP AROUND WHOLE PEELED RIPE BANANAS (1 PER PERSON). PLACE IN A SHALLOW BAKING PAN AND POUR A CHEESE SAUCE OVER THE TOPS. BAKE AT 375°~ 20 MINUTES.

## Maverick Banana Bread

MIX 1 C SUGAR AND 1 CUBE BUTTER. ADD 2 EGGS AND MIX WELL. MASH 3 RIPE BANANAS IN A SEPARATE BOWL AND ADD 2 TBLSP. WATER AND 1 TSP. VANILLA. SIFT 2 C FLOUR, 1/4 TSP. SALT AND 1 TSP. BAKING SODA TOGETHER. ADD ALTERNATELY WITH BANANA MIXTURE TO SUGAR, BUTTER AND EGGS. STIR IN 1/2 C CHOPPED NUTS IF YOU WISH. BAKE IN A GREASED BREAD PAN AT 350° FOR 1 HOUR OR UNTIL DONE.

It's nice to hang a stem of green bananas in the rigging when leaving on a cruise. If they ripen too quickly,

## BANANAS AU RHUM MAY TURN UP FOR

DESSERT: SLICE 1 BANANA PER PERSON INTO A FLAT PAN. COVER WITH A LIGHT LAYER OF BROWN SUGAR (MAVERICK USES MUSCAVADO ~ RAW SUGAR). SPRINKLE WITH LIME JUICE AND LIBERALLY WITH RUM. THIS CONCOCTION SHOULD AGE IN THE REEFER 2 to 3 HOURS. SERVE IN DESSERT CUPS. THERE SHOULD BE ENOUGH SAUCE FOR EACH SERVING TO HAVE A tBLSP. TOP WITH A DOLLOP OF CREAM AND A GRATING OF NUTMEG.

## OR — Flamin' Bananas

PEEL 1 BANANA PER PERSON AND PLACE IN A BUTTERED SHALLOW BAKING DISH. SPRINKLE WITH LIME JUICE, RAW SUGAR AND DOT WITH BUTTER. PLACE IN A 350° OVEN FOR 20 MINUTES (WHILE DINNER'S BEING EATEN). WARM A JIGGER OF RUM PER BANANA TO POUR OVER AND FLAME AT THE TABLE. SPOON SOME SAUCE OVER EACH SERVING.

## Guava-Banana Pie

| | |
|---|---|
| 1 BAKED 9" PIE SHELL | 3 tBLSP. CORNSTARCH |
| 1½ C SLICED RIPE BANANAS | ½ C SUGAR |
| 1½ C GUAVA NECTAR | ¼ tSP. SALT |
| 2 tBLSP. LIME JUICE | 3 tBLSP. WATER |

COMBINE GUAVA NECTAR, LIME JUICE, SUGAR AND SALT. BRING TO A BOIL. MIX CORNSTARCH AND WATER TO A SMOOTH PASTE AND STIR INTO GUAVA MIXTURE. COOK AND STIR TILL IT THICKENS AND TURNS CLEAR. SLICE BANANAS INTO BAKED PIE SHELL AND POUR GUAVA MIX OVER. TOP WITH YOUR FAVORITE MERINGUE AND BROWN AT 325° – 15 MINUTES.

QUICKIES: BANANAS SLICED INTO A BAKED PIE SHELL AND TOPPED WITH PKG. COCONUT CUSTARD, CHOCOLATE OR BUTTERSCOTCH PUDDING ~ SERVE WITH WHIPPED CREAM.

25

 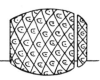

To be at their sweetest, pineapples need to ripen on the stalk ~ not possible for commercially grown ones picked early for shipment. When ripe, a pineapple turns from dark green to a lovely yellow or golden hue and a spine from the top will pull out easily.

①  WAY TO SERVE: Cut a slice from the top, leaving on the leafy crown. Cut off the bottom. With a long thin knife, cut around just inside the shell and push the fruit out. Cut slices lengthwise from all sides to the core. Discard core. Place shell back on bottom and refill with slices. Replace top. Serve with raw sugar on the side for dipping.

## CURRIED SHRIMP IN PINEAPPLE BOATS   (SERVES 6)

| | | |
|---|---|---|
| 1 C COOKED, PEELED SHRIMP | 1 TBLSP. CHOPPED CHIVES | 1¼ C CHICKEN BROTH |
| 2 TBLSP. BUTTER | 2 TOMATOES, CHOPPED | 2 TBLSP. BUTTER |
| 1 CHOPPED ONION | 2 TSP. CURRY PWD. | 2 TBLSP. FLOUR |

### 2 SMALL PINEAPPLES

Sauté in butter onion, 1 tsp. chives and tomatoes. Add curry pwd. and cook 5 minutes. Add chicken broth and shrimp and simmer 5 minutes. Remove from heat. Mix butter and flour and add in bits to sauce. Stir and cook 3 minutes or till thick. Plunge pineapple in boiling water 3 minutes. Drain. Cut in thirds down the middle, leaving spines on. Hollow out some flesh and fill with shrimp. Sprinkle with chives.

### LEFT-OVERS

1. Sauté slices in butter to accompany meats.
2. Pineapple and cheese chunks on toothpics as an appetizer.
3. Sprinkle light rum over slices as a dessert.
4. Chop, sprinkle cointreau over and refrigerate.

### NOTE

The enzymes in fresh pineapple act on gelatin to prevent its thickening. You can heat fresh pineapple to a boil, which kills the enzyme, and then proceed with the gelatin recipe.

## PINEAPPLE BETTY (SERVES 6)

| | | |
|---|---|---|
| 8 SLICES BREAD | 1/3 C RAW SUGAR | CINNAMON AND NUTMEG |
| 2 C CHOPPED PINEAPPLE | 1/4 C BUTTER | WHIPPED CREAM |

TOAST BREAD LIGHTLY. CUT IN CUBES AND SPREAD HALF IN SHALLOW 1 1/2 QT. BAKING DISH. COVER WITH HALF OF PINEAPPLE AND SPRINKLE WITH HALF OF SUGAR. DOT WITH HALF OF BUTTER. REPEAT. SPRINKLE WITH CINNAMON AND NUTMEG. BAKE AT 350° ~ 30 MINUTES. SERVE WARM WITH CREAM.

A PIÑA COLADA IS A DRINK THAT'S BECOME VERY POPULAR IN THE CARIBBEAN IN THE LAST FEW YEARS. HERE'S A DESSERT WITH THE SAME LOVELY FLAVORS.

## PIÑA COLADA SOUFFLÉ (SERVES 6)

SEPARATE 2 EGGS. BEAT YOLKS IN A SAUCEPAN. ADD 1/8 TSP. SALT AND 1 1/4 C PINEAPPLE JUICE, 1/2 C COCONUT CREAM AND 1 TBLSP. UN-FLAVORED GELATIN. HEAT AND STIR ~ SIMMER ABOUT 5 MINUTES TILL SPOON COATS AND THE GELATIN IS DISSOLVED. TAKE FROM HEAT AND ADD 1/4 C RUM. STIR AND CHILL. WHEN MIXTURE MOUNDS ADD THE 2 EGG WHITES, WHICH HAVE BEEN BEATEN STIFF WITH 1 TBLSP. SUGAR. CHILL UNTIL SET. SERVE WITH WHIPPED CREAM OR GRATE NUTMEG OVER THE TOP.

## PAPAYA (PAW-PAW)

PAPAYA IS GOOD FOR YOU. THE FLESH AND LEAVES CONTAIN PAPAIN, USED FOR TENDERIZING MEAT. ITS PEPPERY SEEDS CONTAIN PEPSIN AND MAY BE USED AS CAPERS IN SALADS, ETC. PAPAYA IS A NATIVE OF SOUTH AMERICA AND NOT AT ALL LIKE THE CUSTARD APPLE "PAW PAW" OF THE CENTRAL U.S. SOMETIMES CALLED A TREE-MELON, PAPAYA IS APRICOT COLORED WITH A DELICATE TASTE AND IS COMPLIMENTED WHEN SERVED WITH CITRUS FRUIT. ON MAVERICK, IT'S SLICED LIKE A MELON AND SERVED WITH PIECES OF LIME FOR ACCENT. NATIVES SOMETIMES BOIL PAPAYA GREEN AS A VEGETABLE OR PUT IT IN STEWS AND SOUPS.

# MANGOS

THE TROPICS' ANSWER TO THE PEACH. THERE ARE MANY KINDS GROWN THROUGH THE ISLANDS, VARYING IN SIZE FROM A SMALL PLUM TO A CANTALOUPE AND KNOWN BY AS MANY LOCAL NAMES. WHEN GROWING WILD THEY'RE "TURPENTINE" MANGOS (FOR THE ODOR OF THE CRUSHED LEAVES). THEY HAVE STRINGY FLESH AND ARE BEST FOR MAKING CHUTNEY. IF GRAFTED AND CULTIVATED THEY'RE LIKE GIANT SPICED PEACHES, EASY TO PEEL AND HANDLE ～ JUICY, SMOOTH AND FREE OF FIBRE, THE MORE FAMILIAR ARE "JULIES" OR "BOMBAYS". THE CAPT. WAS FOND OF THE QUOTE : "THE MANGO IS A DELICIOUS AND NOURISHING BREAST-SHAPED DELICACY THAT IS GOD'S WAY OF MAKING MEN OUTGROW THEIR MOTHERS!" THE SKINS ARE NOT EATEN AND THE SAP FROM THE TREE MAY BE IRRITATING. THEY'RE SLOPPY TO EAT, AND TASTE BEST WHEN YOU JUST LEAN OVER AND LET THE JUICE RUN OFF ELBOW AND CHIN. IF YOU MUST BE CIVILIZED, LAY THE MANGO ON ITS FLAT SIDE AND CUT A THICK SLICE FROM BOTH CHEEKS. SCOOP THE MEAT OUT WITH A SPOON OR SCORE FLESH TO THE SKIN, PUSH UP, AND NIP AWAY!

## MANGO PIE

USE MANGOS SLIGHTLY UNDER RIPE. PEEL, SLICE AND SEED MANGOS TO MAKE 4 C. STEAM SLICES IN A LITTLE WATER 20 MINUTES. LINE PIE PAN WITH PASTRY. SPRINKLE ON A GOOD LAYER OF BROWN SUGAR AND A DUSTING OF FLOUR. FILL WITH LAYERS OF FRUIT, DUSTING EACH LAYER WITH A LITTLE FLOUR AND A GENEROUS AMOUNT OF BROWN SUGAR. DOT WITH BUTTER. ADD TOP PASTRY. SEAL EDGES, PRICK CRUST. BAKE AT 375° UNTIL CRUST IS BROWN AND FILLING BUBBLES ---- 30-45 MINUTES. SERVE WARM WITH CREAM. CINNAMON MAY BE ADDED TO THE FILLING IF YOU WISH, AS WELL AS A SQUEEZE OF LIME JUICE.

In the Summertime, when wild MANGOS are dropping from the trees, it's time to make MAVERICK

# CHUTNEY.

| | | |
|---|---|---|
| 18 GREEN MANGOS | 1 LB. RAISINS | 1 TBLSP. SALT |
| 2 LB. RAW SUGAR (IF WHITE, USE LESS) | | ½ SMALL NUTMEG, GRATED |
| 2 PINTS VINEGAR | ½ LB. PRUNES | ¼ TSP. GROUND CLOVES |
| 4 PIECES GREEN GINGER | 4 OZ. MIXED PEEL | 1 TSP. CINNAMON |
| 2 GREEN PEPPERS | 4 MEDIUM ONIONS | 4 SMALL HOT PEPPERS |

WASH AND PEEL MANGOS. CUT IN SMALL PIECES AND BOIL WITH VINEGAR UNTIL TENDER. ADD SUGAR. CHOP FINELY ONIONS, GREEN PEPPERS, PRUNES, HOT PEPPERS, AND ADD TO MANGOS. ADD RAISINS, PEEL, SALT AND SPICES. CRUSH GINGER, TIE IN A MUSLIN BAG AND ADD. BOIL ALL TOGETHER TILL THICK, STIRRING. REMOVE GINGER BAG. BOTTLE IN HOT STERILE JARS AND SEAL WITH PARAFFIN.

## MANGO WHIP    SERVES 4

MASH CANNED OR FRESH MANGOS THROUGH A SIEVE TO MAKE 1 C. ADD THE JUICE OF 1 LIME. BEAT 2 EGG WHITES STIFF AND GRADUALLY ADD ½ C SUGAR AND BEAT TILL STIFF PEAKS FORM. FOLD IN MANGO PULP AND CHILL. FOR A RICHER DESSERT, YOU MAY WHIP ½ C HEAVY CREAM AND FOLD IT INTO THE BEATEN EGG WHITES BEFORE ADDING THE MANGO.

# LIMES

IN THE WEST INDIES, FRESH LIMES ARE AVAILABLE ALL YEAR ROUND. ON BOARD THEY'RE USED WITH ALMOST EVERYTHING ~ FROM BREAKFAST TO THE DESSERT AFTER DINNER. LIMES FOR FISH, SEAFOOD AND SOME MEATS; THEY'RE USED IN VEGETABLES, WITH FRUIT, IN DRESSINGS AND SAUCES. TRY A LITTLE LIME JUICE ON TOP OF PANCAKES AND SYRUP ~ DELICIOUS! PERHAPS BECAUSE MAVERICK IS A BRITISH VESSEL, A KINSHIP IS FELT WITH THOSE EARLY SEAFARING BRITONS WHO WERE LIMEYS TOO.

LIME ICING ~ MIX 3 TBLSP. BUTTER, 2 TO 3 C PWD. SUGAR, THE JUICE AND GRATES OF 2 LIMES AND ENOUGH WATER FOR PROPER CONSISTENCY. IF IT DOESN'T LOOK LIMEY ENOUGH FOR YOU, ADD A DROP OF GREEN FOOD COLORING.

## Lime Sauce (FOR CAKES OR PUDDINGS, ETC.)

MIX ½ C SUGAR, ⅛ tSP. SALT AND 2 tBLSP. CORN-STARCH IN A SAUCEPAN. GRADUALLY StIR IN 1 C BOILING WATER. COOK UNtiL tHICK AND CLEAR. REMOVE FROM HEAt AND StIR IN 2 tBLSP. BUttER AND tHE JUICE AND GRAtES OF 2 LIMES. ADD A DROP OF GREEN FOOD COLORING IF YOU WISH. MAKES 1¾ C. GOOD ON GINGERBREAD.

### LIME JELLY

(MAKES 5 - 8 OZ. GLASSES)

1 PKG. (2 OZ.) PWD. FRUit PECtIN
2 C WAtER          1 C LIME JUICE
3¾ C SUGAR    GREEN FOOD COLOR

COMBINE PECtIN, WATER AND LIME JUICE IN A KEttLE. COOK RAPIDLY, StIRRING, UNtIL BUBBLES FORM AROUND EDGE OF POt. StIR IN SUGAR. COOK, StIRRING, 2 MIN-UtES OR JUSt UNtIL SUGAR DISSOLVES. (DO NOT BOIL). REMOVE FROM HEAt. LIGHtLY tINt WItH GREEN; SKIM. POUR INtO HOt StERILIZED JARS AND SEAL WItH PARAFIN.

### LIME RIND JAM

GRIND 3 C LIME RINDS AND PULP (AFTER SQUEEZING) WItH tHE FINE BLADE OF tHE MEAt GRINDER. COVER WItH WAtER IN A KEttLE AND ADD ⅛ tSP. BAKING SODA. BRING tO A BOIL AND SIMMER, COVERED, 20 MINUtES. DRAIN. ADD 1½ C WAtER AND 5 C SUGAR. BOIL 20-25 MINUtES OR tILL MIXtURE SHEEtS WHEN DROPPED FROM A SPOON. POUR INtO HOt StERILIZED JARS AND SEAL WItH PARAFIN.

## Lime Soufflé (SERVES 8)

| 1 C SUGAR | 2 tBLSP. MELtED BUttER | ½ C MILK |
| 4 tBLSP. FLOUR | GRAtED RINDS 2 LIMES | 3 EGG YOLKS, BEATEN |
| ⅛ tSP. SALt | 5 tBLSP. LIME JUICE | 3 EGG WHItES, StIFFLY BEATEN |

BLEND SUGAR, FLOUR, SALt, BUttER, LIME JUICE, RIND, YOLKS AND MILK. FOLD IN WHItES. POUR INtO WELL-GREASED BAKING DISH. PUt IN PAN OF HOt WAtER AND BAKE At 350° FOR 1 HOUR. SERVE HOt OR COLD WItH WHIPPED CREAM.

30

## Key Lime Pie

SEPARATE 4 EGGS. BEAT YOLKS UNTIL VERY LIGHT. ADD 1 CAN (15 oz.) SWEETENED CONDENSED MILK. BEAT TILL VERY LIGHT.... BEAT, BEAT! ADD ½ - ⅔ C LIME JUICE, BEATING UNTIL THICK. POUR INTO BAKED AND COOLED 9" PIE CRUST AND TOP WITH MERINGUE, WHIPPED CREAM OR SOUR CREAM. CHILL.

# Other Tropical Fruits

TAMARIND – LOOKS LIKE A BROWN BULBOUS BEAN. IN- SIDE IS A PULP THAT TASTES LIKE A DRY MEALY APRI- COT, WITH A SHARPER FLAVOR. IT'S USED VERY OFTEN IN CHUTNEYS, MAKES A TART REFRESHING DRINK AND A NICE JAM. YOU CAN BUY CANNED "TAMARINDO" JUICE IN PUERTO RICO.

GENIP- IS A PLENTIFUL SMALL GREEN FRUIT. CRACK THE SHELL WITH YOUR TEETH AND THERE'S PEACH-COLORED FLESH AROUND A LARGE STONE. IT'S PUCKERY AND THIRST-QUENCHING. WEST INDIANS PICK BUNCHES AND SUCK ON THEM AS THEY GO ABOUT THEIR BUSINESS. SO DO WE! BOILED UP, STRAINED AND SUGARED TO TASTE ~ A DELICIOUS DRINK.

SOURSOP ~ AN UNUSUAL GREEN KIDNEY-SHAPED PRICKLY FRUIT. THE SWEET-SOUR JUICE EXTRACTED FROM ITS WHITE PULP MAKES A COOLING DRINK WITH A "GREEN" TASTE. IT'S ALSO USED TO MAKE ICE CREAM AND A SOURSOP DAIQUIRI IS SOMETHING YOU WOULDN'T FORGET. IT, TOO, IS CANNED IN PUERTO RICO. THE SPANISH NAME IS "GUANABANA".

31

CASHEW — THE NUT IS POISONOUS UNTIL ROASTED. IT'S ATTACHED TO A REDDISH OR YELLOW PEAR-SHAPED FRUIT, FROM WHICH YOU MAY SUCK THE JUICE. SLIGHTLY PUCKERY, BUT REFRESHING AS YOU WALK IN THE COUNTRY.

SUGAR APPLE

A FRUIT MADE UP OF SORT OF KNOBS AND WHEN RIPE AND SOFT, CAN BE PULLED APART AND THE SWEET WHITE PULP EATEN RAW.

GUAVA — THE GUAVA IS CULTIVATED THROUGHOUT THE TROPICS FOR ITS DELICIOUS JAMS, PASTES, JELLIES AND THE JUICE MADE FROM THE WHITE OR PINK PULP. CANNED PUERTO RICAN GUAVA NECTAR IS OFTEN USED ON MAVERICK, AS WELL AS GUAVA PASTE (SERVED WITH COUNTRY CHEESE AS AN APPETIZER) AND GUAVA SHELLS (FILL WITH CREAM CHEESE FOR A DESSERT).

SEA GRAPE — THESE BUSHES ARE FOUND AT THE TOP OF MOST WEST INDIAN BEACHES AND PRO-DUCE A DARK RED GRAPE THAT MAY BE EATEN, THOUGH THERE'S NOT MUCH TO THEM COMPARED TO NORTHERN GRAPES. THEY DO MAKE A NICE JELLY OR JAM.

THEN THERE'S THE SAPODILLA, A ROUGH BROWN FRUIT FROM THE CHICKLE TREE (THE SAP IS USED TO MAKE CHEWING GUM). IT'S USED RAW IN FRUIT CUP AND SALADS AND IS OFTEN MADE INTO PRESERVES OR SYRUP. AND MAMMEE APPLES~ ROUND THICK-SKINNED BROWN FRUITS WITH ORANGE FLESH. THEY CAN BE EATEN RAW OR COOKED, AND HAVE THE STRANGEST LARGE OBLONG BUMPY SEEDS.

32

# Manchineel XXXX

MUST BE MENTIONED AS IT IS FOUND SO FREQUENTLY ALONG
BEACHES IN THE WEST INDIES. THE MANCHINEEL TREE HAS
SMALL GREEN APPLES WHICH SMELL A BIT LIKE CRABAPPLES.
BUT YOU MUST BEWARE! IT'S THE PROVERBIAL POISON APPLE
AND CAN BE DEADLY. EVEN TO SHELTER UNDER ITS BRANCHES
IN A RAIN WILL IRRITATE YOUR SKIN. IT IS SAID THE CARIB INDIANS USED
MANCHINEEL TO POISON THEIR ENEMIES.

CERTO AND EXTRA SUGAR ARE ALWAYS CARRIED ALONG ON MAVERICK
IN CASE SOME RIPE FRUIT TURNS UP WHILE EXPLORING ASHORE. EVEN
WITHOUT A RECIPE, THE FRUIT IS BOILED UP, SUGAR, LIME AND CERTO
ADDED AND ~ PRESTO! ~ A FEW JARS OF JAM (OR SYRUP) FOR THE TABLE.
WHEN THE GALLEY GETS TOO HOT — THE COOK TAKES A PLUNGE!

# AVOCADO

AVOCADOS ORIGINATED IN LATIN AMERICA
AND ARE CALLED "PEARS" THROUGH MOST OF
THE ENGLISH SPEAKING CARIBBEAN. THEY'RE PLENTIFUL IN THE
SUMMER AND SO GOOD JUST AS THEY COME, WITH LIME AND SALT.    SOME FOLKS
LIKE THEM FILLED WITH A FAVORITE FRENCH DRESSING, OR SHRIMP. MASH THEM
AND SPREAD ON BREAD FOR A CHICKEN OR HAM SANDWICH. TRY SLICING THEM
WITH ALTERNATE GRAPEFRUIT SECTIONS ON A BED OF BIBB LETTUCE. (WITH FRENCH
DRESSING).

## Maverick Guacamole

| | | |
|---|---|---|
| 1 RIPE AVOCADO | 1 TSP. FINELY CHOPPED ONION | DASH TABASCO |
| 2 TSP. LIME JUICE | 1/8 TSP. SALT | 3 TBLSP. MAYONNAISE |
| 1 TSP. WORCESTERSHIRE | DASH PEPPER | PAPRIKA |

MASH AVOCADO AND ADD EVERYTHING EXCEPT PAPRIKA. BLEND WELL. PUT AVO-
CADO STONE BACK IN MIXTURE (PREVENTS DISCOLORATION). REMOVE STONE
BEFORE SERVING. SPRINKLE WITH PAPRIKA. IF YOU HAVE SOUR CREAM,
YOU MAY WISH TO USE IT INSTEAD OF THE MAYONNAISE.

33

# ZULU
## AVOCADO SOUP

| 1 CAN CR. MUSHROOM SOUP **OR** 1 CAN CR. OF CHICKEN SOUP | MILK | 2 tSP. GRATED ONION |
|---|---|---|
| | 1 PINT SOUR CREAM | 1 tBLSP. WORCESTER-SHIRE |
| 2 MASHED, RIPE AVOCADOS | 1 tBLSP. LIME JUICE | SALT AND PEPPER |

MIX ALL tOGETHER, USING JUST ENOUGH MILK tO MAKE tHE PROPER CONSIS-TENCY. ADD SALt AND PEPPER tO tASTE. CHILL At LEAST 2 HOURS BEFORE SERVING. GARNISH WITH A DAB OF SOUR CREAM. SERVES 8.

# ☞ PUMPKIN

PUMPKINS IN tHE ISLANDS AREN't tHE SAME AS HALLOWEEN PUMPKINS IN tHE StATES. ISLAND PUMPKINS ARE USUALLY MOttLED GREEN AND WHITE AND COME IN ALL SHAPES AND SIZES. NORTHERN PUMPKINS MAY BE USED IN tHE SAME WAY OR HUBBARD SQUASH WOULD DO AS WELL. MAVERICK HAD WESt INDIAN COOKS FOR MANY YEARS. FERNANDO IS FROM St. LUCIA AND tURNED OUt tHOUSANDS OF DELICIOUS MEALS FOR MAVERICK'S tABLE. ONE OF HIS BESt RECIPES IS:

### FERNANDO'S PUMPKIN SOUP (SERVES 8-10)

PEEL 2-2½ LB. PUMPKIN, SCRAPE OUt tHE SEEDS, CUt IN CHUNKS AND BOIL IN SALtED WATER UNTIL tENDER. DRAIN, RESERVING WATER AND MASH PUMPKIN FINE. ADD PUMPKIN WATER (OR CHICKEN OR BEEF BROtH) UNTIL A tHICK PUREE. ADD 2 CHOPPED CARROTS, 1 DICED StALK CELERY, 3 SLICES CHOPPED BACON, 1 LG. CHOPPED ONION, 1 CHOPPED GREEN PEPPER. SIMMER UNTIL VEGEtABLES ARE tENDER. ADD 1 tBLSP. FLOUR (MIXED tO A PASTE WITH WATER), ½ tSP. tHYME, 1 C CANNED tOMATOES (OR CHOPPED FRESH), SALt AND PEP-PER tO tASTE AND A DAB OF BUttER. HEAt ½ CAN EVAPORATED MILK AND ADD JUSt BEFORE SERVING. FERNANDO CHOPS FRESH PARSLEY ON tOP BEFORE DISHING UP. It'S GOOD WITH SEASONED tOASt.

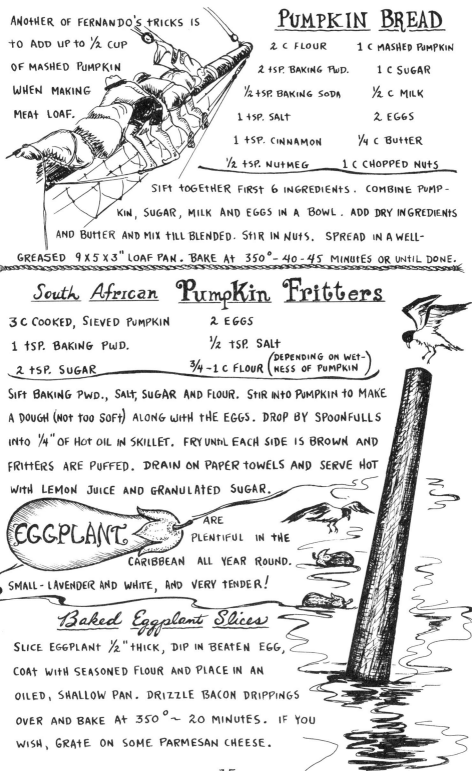

ANOTHER OF FERNANDO'S TRICKS IS TO ADD UP TO ½ CUP OF MASHED PUMPKIN WHEN MAKING MEAT LOAF.

# PUMPKIN BREAD

| | |
|---|---|
| 2 C FLOUR | 1 C MASHED PUMPKIN |
| 2 tSP. BAKING PWD. | 1 C SUGAR |
| ½ tSP. BAKING SODA | ½ C MILK |
| 1 tSP. SALT | 2 EGGS |
| 1 tSP. CINNAMON | ¼ C BUTTER |
| ½ tSP. NUTMEG | 1 C CHOPPED NUTS |

SIFT TOGETHER FIRST 6 INGREDIENTS. COMBINE PUMPKIN, SUGAR, MILK AND EGGS IN A BOWL. ADD DRY INGREDIENTS AND BUTTER AND MIX TILL BLENDED. STIR IN NUTS. SPREAD IN A WELL-GREASED 9 X 5 X 3" LOAF PAN. BAKE AT 350° - 40-45 MINUTES OR UNTIL DONE.

## South African Pumpkin Fritters

| | |
|---|---|
| 3 C COOKED, SIEVED PUMPKIN | 2 EGGS |
| 1 tSP. BAKING PWD. | ½ tSP. SALT |
| 2 tSP. SUGAR | ¾ -1 C FLOUR (DEPENDING ON WET-NESS OF PUMPKIN) |

SIFT BAKING PWD., SALT, SUGAR AND FLOUR. STIR INTO PUMPKIN TO MAKE A DOUGH (NOT TOO SOFT) ALONG WITH THE EGGS. DROP BY SPOONFULLS INTO ¼" OF HOT OIL IN SKILLET. FRY UNTIL EACH SIDE IS BROWN AND FRITTERS ARE PUFFED. DRAIN ON PAPER TOWELS AND SERVE HOT WITH LEMON JUICE AND GRANULATED SUGAR.

EGGPLANT ARE PLENTIFUL IN THE CARIBBEAN ALL YEAR ROUND. SMALL - LAVENDER AND WHITE, AND VERY TENDER!

### Baked Eggplant Slices

SLICE EGGPLANT ½" THICK, DIP IN BEATEN EGG, COAT WITH SEASONED FLOUR AND PLACE IN AN OILED, SHALLOW PAN. DRIZZLE BACON DRIPPINGS OVER AND BAKE AT 350° ~ 20 MINUTES. IF YOU WISH, GRATE ON SOME PARMESAN CHEESE.

## Stuffed Eggplant (SERVES 12)

CUT 6 SMALL EGGPLANT IN HALF LENGTHWISE. SCOOP OUT FLESH AND DICE. SAUTÉ 1 CHOPPED ONION, 1 MASHED CLOVE GARLIC, AND 1 CHOPPED GREEN PEPPER IN BUTTER. ADD EGGPLANT AND STIR-FRY UNTIL THE EGGPLANT SOFTENS. BREAK UP 2 SLICES OF BREAD AND ADD. IF THERE'S A TOMATO AROUND, CHOP IT AND ADD TO THE ABOVE. SPRINKLE WITH A LITTLE PIC-A-PEPPER OR HOT SAUCE. STIR. REFILL SHELLS AND SPRINKLE BUTTERED BREAD CRUMBS ON TOP. REHEAT IN A 350° OVEN FOR 20 MINUTES BEFORE SERVING.

# BREADFRUIT

THE BREADFRUIT TREE WAS INTRODUCED INTO JAMAICA AND ST. VINCENT IN 1793 BY CAPT. BLIGH, WHO BROUGHT IT FROM TAHITI. SINCE THEN, IT HAS SPREAD THROUGH THE REST OF THE CARIBBEAN. ITS FRUIT IS EITHER FRIED, ROASTED OR BOILED AND IT HAS A FAIRLY BLAND, POTATO-LIKE TASTE. WE LIKE CHIPS THAT HAVE BEEN DEEP FRIED AND SALTED. FERNANDO MAKES FANTASTIC CROQUETTES BY MASHING COOKED BREADFRUIT WITH MILK, BUTTER AND SEASONINGS, DIPPING MOUNDS IN EGG AND CRUMBS AND FRYING THEM UNTIL GOLDEN. ITS GOOD FIXED AS POTATO SALAD. IF YOU'RE A BREADFRUIT FIEND, YOU'LL WANT IT COOKED, AND BUTTERED AND SALTED.

## BREADNUTS ↦ ARE A SMALLER, SEEDED VARIETY OF BREADFRUIT.

THE OUTSIDE SKIN LOOKS THE SAME, BUT HAS SPINELIKE PROJECTIONS. THE NUTS ARE EMBEDDED IN THE FLESH. RATHER LIKE CHESTNUTS, THEY'RE USED IN THE SAME WAY. THEY'RE BOILED IN SALTED WATER UNTIL TENDER. WEST INDIANS PUT THEM IN SOUPS AND STUFFINGS. COOKED BREADNUTS FRIED IN BUTTER AND SALTED MAKE A FINE SNACK AT COCKTAIL TIME.

# Christophene
### Chayote in Mexico and California

THIS IS A PALE GREEN OR CREAM-COLORED, PEAR-SHAPED VEGETABLE FURROWED AND SLIGHTLY PRICKLY. IT'S FOUND IN CALIFORNIA, THROUGH MEXICO, CENTRAL AMERICA AND THE CARIBBEAN. IT'S FLAVOR IS DELICATE AND SIMILAR TO THAT OF A LIGHT SUMMER SQUASH. SUGGESTED USES:

1. STEAM AND DRAIN SLICED CHRISTOPHENE — SERVE WITH BUTTER, SALT AND PEPPER.

2. STEAM, DRAIN AND SERVE SLICED CHRISTOPHENE WITH A CREAM OR CHEESE SAUCE.

3. SAUTÉ ONION, GREEN PEPPER AND A CHOPPED TOMATO. MIX IN COOKED SLICES OF CHRISTOPHENE AND SEASON WITH SALT, PEPPER, SEASON-ALL AND BUTTER. SPRINKLE WITH PARMESAN CHEESE.

4. STEAM, DRAIN, CHILL AND USE IN SALADS.

## STUFFED CHRISTOPHENE

| | |
|---|---|
| 3 CHRISTOPHENE | 1 C BUTTERED BREAD CRUMBS |
| 2 TBLSP. BUTTER | 1 C GRATED CHEDDAR CHEESE |
| SALT AND PEPPER | CELERY SALT |
| ½ MINCED ONION | SEASON-ALL |

WASH CHRISTOPHENE, CUT IN HALF LENGTHWISE AND BOIL IN SALTED WATER UNTIL TENDER. COOL. REMOVE SEEDS WITH A TBLSP. SCOOP OUT FLESH, KEEPING SHELLS INTACT. MASH FLESH WITH SALT, PEPPER, CELERY SALT AND SEASON-ALL TO TASTE. ADD BUTTER, THEN CHEESE. ADD BREAD CRUMBS. MIX WELL AND SPOON BACK INTO SHELLS. PLACE IN A SHALLOW BAKING PAN AND SPRINKLE WITH ADDITIONAL BREAD CRUMBS. BAKE AT 350° FOR 25 MINUTES. SERVES 6.

**Other** VEGETABLES USED ON MAVERICK MAY NOT BE QUITE SO EXOTIC. THE LOWLY  **CARROT** IS ALWAYS ON HAND. IT TURNS UP IN SOUPS, STEWS AND SALADS. SOMETIMES IT'S EVEN SERVED AS A VEGETABLE!

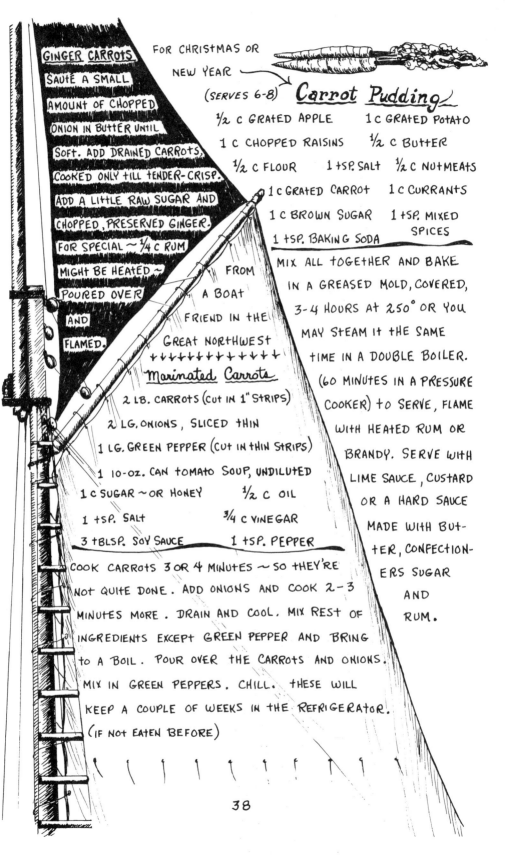

## GINGER CARROTS

SAUTÉ A SMALL AMOUNT OF CHOPPED ONION IN BUTTER UNTIL SOFT. ADD DRAINED CARROTS, COOKED ONLY TILL TENDER-CRISP. ADD A LITTLE RAW SUGAR AND CHOPPED, PRESERVED GINGER. FOR SPECIAL ~ 1/4 C RUM MIGHT BE HEATED ~ POURED OVER AND FLAMED.

FOR CHRISTMAS OR NEW YEAR ~

(SERVES 6-8)

## Carrot Pudding

1/2 C GRATED APPLE    1 C GRATED POTATO

1 C CHOPPED RAISINS    1/2 C BUTTER

1/2 C FLOUR    1 tSP. SALT    1/2 C NUTMEATS

1 C GRATED CARROT    1 C CURRANTS

1 C BROWN SUGAR    1 tSP. MIXED SPICES

1 tSP. BAKING SODA

MIX ALL TOGETHER AND BAKE IN A GREASED MOLD, COVERED, 3-4 HOURS AT 250° OR YOU MAY STEAM IT THE SAME TIME IN A DOUBLE BOILER. (60 MINUTES IN A PRESSURE COOKER) TO SERVE, FLAME WITH HEATED RUM OR BRANDY. SERVE WITH LIME SAUCE, CUSTARD OR A HARD SAUCE MADE WITH BUTTER, CONFECTIONERS SUGAR AND RUM.

FROM A BOAT FRIEND IN THE GREAT NORTHWEST

+ + + + + + + + + + + +

## Marinated Carrots

2 LB. CARROTS (CUT IN 1" STRIPS)

2 LG. ONIONS, SLICED THIN

1 LG. GREEN PEPPER (CUT IN THIN STRIPS)

1 10-OZ. CAN TOMATO SOUP, UNDILUTED

1 C SUGAR ~ OR HONEY    1/2 C OIL

1 tSP. SALT    3/4 C VINEGAR

3 tBLSP. SOY SAUCE    1 tSP. PEPPER

COOK CARROTS 3 OR 4 MINUTES ~ SO THEY'RE NOT QUITE DONE. ADD ONIONS AND COOK 2-3 MINUTES MORE. DRAIN AND COOL. MIX REST OF INGREDIENTS EXCEPT GREEN PEPPER AND BRING TO A BOIL. POUR OVER THE CARROTS AND ONIONS. MIX IN GREEN PEPPERS. CHILL. THESE WILL KEEP A COUPLE OF WEEKS IN THE REFRIGERATOR. (IF NOT EATEN BEFORE)

$\mathcal{T}$HERE ARE MANY ROOT VEGETABLES, WHICH ARE CALLED "GROUND PROVISIONS". IRISH POTATOES ARE SHIPPED IN, BUT THE LOCAL NATIVE MARKETS HAVE PILES OF OTHER ROUGH-LOOKING ROOTS ~ SOME HAIRY, COVERED WITH DIRT AND IN MANY SHAPES AND SIZES. ALL ARE EDIBLE STARCHES. CASSAVA IS A THIN ROOT CONTAINING PRUSSIC ACID THAT HAS TO BE BOILED OR ROASTED TO EXTRACT THE POISON BEFORE USING. WHEN GROUND INTO A FLOUR, IT'S USED FOR CASSAVA BREAD OR OTHER FARINA DISHES. THERE ARE YUCCA, TANNIA, DASHEEN (OR EDDOE), SWEET POTATOES AND YAMS. ALL ARE FIXED AS POTATOES AND INTERESTING TO TRY. DASHEEN IS THE SAME AS TARO IN THE SOUTH PACIFIC. IT'S STARCH IS ALKALINE INSTEAD OF ACID.

$\mathcal{O}$NE OF THE COOKS WAS FROM St. VINCENT AND HE MADE A SWEET POTATO BREAD (MORE A STIFF PUDDING) FOR TEA TIME:

### E.J.'s SWEET POTATO BREAD

GRATE (VERY FINE) 6 SWEET POTATOES. ADD 1/4 C MILK, 1/4 C SUGAR (OR TO TASTE), 2 TBLSP. BUTTER, A DASH OF CINNAMON, A DASH OF ALLSPICE, AND 1/2 - 3/4 C FLOUR. YOU MAY ADD A FEW RAISINS, 1/2 CAN COCONUT (OR 1 FRESH COCONUT, GRATED) MIX ALL AND BAKE AT 350° IN A LARGE, BUTTERED RECTANGULAR PAN FOR 45 MINUTES. SERVE WARM. SERVES 12.

$\mathcal{A}$LTHOUGH AS MANY FRESH SUPPLIES AS POSSIBLE ARE TAKEN ON CRUISES, CANS ARE DEPENDED UPON TO SUPPLEMENT AND EXTEND MENUS. HARDLY ANYTHING CANNED IS SERVED WITHOUT DRESSING IT UP SOMEHOW. HERE'S ONE WAY TO FIX CANNED YAMS — TO SERVE WITH HAM:

### Sherried Yams ~ DRAIN 3 - #2 1/2 CANS YAMS, SAVING LIQUID.

MASH YAMS AND ADD: 1/4 C MELTED BUTTER, 1 TSP. SALT, 2 BEATEN EGGS, 1/4 C SHERRY, 1/4 C ORANGE JUICE, 1/4 TSP. GINGER, 1/2 TSP. CINNAMON, AND 1 TSP. GRATED ORANGE PEEL. MIX WELL. IF MORE LIQUID IS NEEDED, ADD DRAINED JUICE. SMOOTH INTO BUTTERED PANS AND SPRINKLE WITH 1/2 C CHOPPED WALNUTS. BAKE AT 350° - 1/2 - 3/4 HOUR. (SERVES 10)

**B**efore LEAVING VEGETABLES, A WORD MUST BE SAID ABOUT <u>CALLALOO</u>. CALLALOO IS THE LEAF FROM THE DASHEEN ROOT AND IS SIMILAR TO SPINACH ~ WITH A MUCH LARGER LEAF. IT IS BEST KNOWN IN THE CARIBBEAN FOR A SOUP CALLED "CALLALOO." THERE ARE AS MANY WAYS TO FIX CALALOO AS THERE ARE ISLANDS. HERE'S OUR QUICK 'N EASY VERSION:

## MAVERICK CALLALOO

2 SLICES BACON, DICED

1 SMALL MINCED ONION

1 - 13 ¾ OZ. CAN CHICKEN BROTH

1 - 10 OZ. PKG. CHOPPED FROZEN SPINACH

1 - 13 OZ. CAN CRAB SOUP MARYLAND

⅓ C COCONUT CREAM      ¼ TSP. THYME      ¼ TSP. GARLIC SALT

DASH PEPPER      1 TBLSP. WORCESTERSHIRE      1 TBLSP. PIC-A-PEPPER SAUCE

1 TBLSP. BUTTER      1 TBLSP. PARSLEY

SAUTÉ BACON AND ONION UNTIL THE ONION IS SOFT. ADD CHICKEN BROTH AND SPINACH. SIMMER UNTIL SPINACH IS TENDER. ADD CRAB SOUP (CROSS AND BLACK-WELL). PUT THROUGH A SIEVE OR WHIR IN A BLENDER UNTIL SMOOTH. RETURN TO THE POT AND ADD REMAINING INGREDIENTS. HEAT AND SERVE GARNISHED WITH A LITTLE PIMIENTO OR A DAB OF SOUR CREAM. SERVES 6.

**T**HERE'S ALMOST ALWAYS SOMEONE ON BOARD WHO'S INTERESTED IN COLLECTING SHELLS. THE WEST INDIAN TOP — LOCALLY CALLED "WHELK", LIVES ON ROCKS JUST AT THE TIDE LINE. THEY'RE OUR ESCARGOT AND ARE STEAMED IN SEA WATER TO SERVE HOT AT COCKTAIL TIME WITH GARLIC BUTTER.

## *TORTOLA WHELK FRITTERS*

STEAMED WHELK ARE GROUND AND MIXED WITH A BATTER (JUST ENOUGH TO HOLD THEM TOGETHER) OF BISQUICK MIXED WITH BEER. ADD A TOUCH OF WORCESTERSHIRE AND HOT SAUCE. DROP BY TSP. IN HOT OIL AND FRY TILL BROWN. SERVE WITH TARTARE OR COCKTAIL SAUCE. YOU MAY TRY MINCED CLAMS IN PLACE OF THE WHELK.

40

If THE SHELL COLLECTORS (OR SEA-FOOD LOVERS) HAVE BEEN DILIGENT AND THERE ARE MORE WHELK THAN CAN BE USED FOR APPETIZERS,

## *Whelk and Rice* MAY APPEAR FOR LUNCH.

STEAM WHELK AND GRIND ENOUGH TO MAKE 1 C. COOK 1 C RAW RICE IN 2 C CHICKEN BROTH 25 MINUTES. SAUTÉ 2 SLICES CHOPPED BACON. ADD 1 LG. CHOPPED ONION, 1 MINCED CLOVE GARLIC, 1 TBLSP. CHOPPED PARSLEY, ½ TSP. OREGANO, AND THE WHELK. STIR-FRY TILL THE ONION IS SOFT. REMOVE FROM HEAT AND ADD ¼ C WHITE WINE AND 1 TBLSP. WORCESTERSHIRE. MIX WITH RICE. ADD SALT AND PEPPER IF NEEDED. SPRINKLE WITH PARMESAN CHEESE BEFORE SERVING. AGAIN ~ YOU MAY SUBSTITUTE CLAMS FOR WHELK. SERVES 4-6.

AND SPEAKING OF CLAMS, CANNED MINCED CLAMS ARE ALWAYS IN THE LOCKER AND USED FOR A VARIETY OF DIFFERENT DISHES. HERE ARE A FEW: ## CLAM CAKES (FOR 3)

| | |
|---|---|
| 2 EGGS, BEATEN | ¼ TSP. SALT |
| 1-8 OZ. CAN MINCED CLAMS, UNDRAINED | DASH PEPPER |
| 1 C FINE ROLLED SALTINE CRACKERS | 3 TBLSP. BACON DRIPPINGS |

COMBINE FIRST 5 INGREDIENTS. DROP BY TBLSP. IN HOT BACON GREASE IN SKILLET. BROWN BOTH SIDES. MAKES 6. SERVE WITH TARTARE SAUCE.

## Clam Sauce for Spaghetti

HEAT 2 TBLSP. OLIVE OIL IN SKILLET. ADD A FEW SPRIGS OF PARSLEY, CHOPPED, 1 MINCED CLOVE GARLIC, AND 1 FINE-CHOPPED MEDIUM ONION. SAUTÉ UNTIL ONION IS SOFT. ADD ½ TSP. SALT, A DASH OF PEPPER AND 1-8 OZ. CAN OF UNDRAINED MINCED CLAMS. HEAT AND ADD ⅓ C DRY WHITE WINE. DO NOT BOIL. MAKES ENOUGH FOR 1 LB. SPAGHETTI.

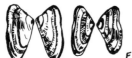

# Clam Chowder

FRY UP 2 SLICES CHOPPED BACON, 2 CHOPPED MEDIUM ONIONS, 2 CHOPPED MEDIUM POTATOES. WHEN SLIGHTLY BROWN, ADD 2 CANS CHICKEN BROTH AND SIMMER UNTIL POTATOES ARE TENDER. ADD 1 CAN CREAM CORN, THE JUICE FROM 2 CANS MINCED CLAMS, 1 TBLSP. WORCESTERSHIRE, SALT AND PEPPER TO TASTE. ADD ½ - 1 CAN EVAPORATED MILK, 1 TBLSP. PARSLEY, 2 TBLSP. BUTTER. HEAT AND ADD RESERVED CLAMS. SERVES 10.

PERHAPS THE MOST IMPRESSIVE OF THE CARIBBEAN SEASHELLS IS THE **QUEEN CONCH** THIS GIANT MOLLUSK IS COLLECTED NOT ONLY FOR ITS LOVELY PINK AND ORANGE COLOR, BUT FOR THE MEAT OF THE ANIMAL WHO BUILDS IT. CONCH HAS LONG BEEN A STAPLE OF THE WEST INDIAN DIET. IT'S QUITE A DELICACY TO SEA FOOD LOVERS AND ANYONE WHO GOES THROUGH THE JOB OF PREPARING CONCH, STARTING FROM THE LIVE FELLA STILL IN THE SHELL, CAN DOUBLY APPRECIATE THE END RESULT. HOW YOU REMOVE SIR CONCH FROM HIS SHELL, CLEAN OFF HIS SLIME, TRIM AND POUND HIM ~ IS A BOOK UNTO ITSELF. * THESE RECIPES ARE FOR CONCH AFTER THESE PRELIMINARIES. IN PUERTO RICO, THE GOYA CO. HAS A CANNED CONCH (CARRUCHO) WHICH MAY BE USED IN MANY WAYS ~ OF COURSE, <u>NOT</u> AS GOOD AS THE FRESH.....! CONCH MAY BE SIMMERED IN WATER ABOUT 1½ HOURS OR PRESSURE COOKED 30 MINUTES.

## CONCH FRITTERS

BOIL POUNDED CONCH TILL TENDER. GRIND WITH THE MEDIUM BLADE OF THE MEAT GRINDER. ADD CHOPPED ONION AND GREEN PEPPER. MIX IN SOME BISQUICK AND FLAT BEER UNTIL MOIST. (BATTER AT A MINIMUM – MOSTLY CONCH). ADD A SMALL AMOUNT OF PIC-A-PEPPER SAUCE AND WORCESTERSHIRE AND CELERY SALT. DROP BY TSP. INTO HOT OIL AND BROWN ON EACH SIDE. SERVE WITH TARTARE OR COCKTAIL SAUCE. AN EASY <u>COCKTAIL SAUCE:</u> MIX CATSUP WITH A LITTLE LIME JUICE, A SLOP OF WORCESTERSHIRE, SALT, PEPPER AND A DASH OF HOT SAUCE. YOU MAY TRY CANNED CLAMS IN PLACE OF THE CONCH, BUT IT WON'T BE THE SAME!

* SEE "THE CONCH BOOK" © 1982 DEE CARSTARPHEN, PEN & INK PRESS, DISTRIBUTED BY BANYAN BOOKS.

# INGA'S CONCH CHOWDER

CUT 4 CONCHS IN PIECES. PRESSURE COOK 30 MINUTES IN WATER, SALT AND 6 SMALL CHICKEN BOUILLON CUBES. SAUTÉ 3 ONIONS AND 2 CUBED, COOKED POTATOES. ADD A COUPLE OF COOKED, SLICED CARROTS FOR COLOR, THE CONCH, SALT AND PEPPER, PARSLEY AND A SPLASH OF WHITE WINE. AT THE LAST MINUTE, ADD A CAN OF EVAPORATED MILK.

A FRIEND IN ST. THOMAS WHO RUNS A FISHING BOAT DREAMED UP THIS SHORT-CUT CHOWDER ~ JACK'S 1-2-3 CONCH CHOWDER (SERVES 4) 1. 1 CAN (10½ OZ.) GOYA CONCH (DRAIN) 2. 1 CAN (1 LB.) REEDS GERMAN POTATO SALAD 3. 1 CAN (1 LB.) STEWED TOMATOES (WITH SPICES). MIX ALL TOGETHER AND HEAT. IF TOO THICK, THIN WITH CHICKEN BROTH. MAVERICK HAS USED A CHOWDER RECIPE THAT TAKES ABOUT 2 HOURS TO PREPARE ~ VERY MUCH THE SAME.

## De Coteau's Conch

JOE DE COTEAU IS FROM DOMINICA. HIS CONCH WAS SERVED WITH RICE OR AS A SHORT COURSE: COVER 6 CONCH WITH WATER AND BOIL HARD ½ HR. DRAIN. CHOP ½ TOMATO, ½ ONION, ½ GREEN PEPPER AND SAUTE IN 2 TSP. OIL. ADD CONCH, ¾ TSP. BLACK PEPPER, 2 TSP. WORCESTERSHIRE, AND ¼ TSP. HEINZ BROWNING. ADD A LITTLE CURRY PWD. IF YOU WISH. MIX AND STIR-FRY A COUPLE OF MINUTES. ADD WATER TO COVER. ADD SALT IF NEEDED, ¼ TSP. THYME AND 1 TBLSP. BUTTER. SIMMER TILL THE WATER IS ALMOST GONE AND THE SAUCE IS THICK.

**CONCH LAMBI:** GRIND COOKED CONCH ON THE MEDIUM BLADE OF THE MEAT GRINDER AND MIX WITH CHOPPED HARD BOILED EGG, A LITTLE MINCED GREEN PEPPER, BLACK PEPPER, LIME JUICE AND A TOUCH OF SALT. SERVE ON LETTUCE AS A SHORT COURSE.

**Conch Salad:** GRIND RAW POUNDED CONCH AND ONION, GREEN PEPPER, AND PIMIENTO. MARINATE ALL IN LIME JUICE AT LEAST 3 HOURS. SEASON WITH SALT AND TABASCO.

A COUPLE OF "BEWARES" FOR SNORKLERS WHO YEN to COLLECT SHELLS AND MIGHT HANDLE STRANGE THINGS UNDERWATER. WEAR A GLOVE! FIRE CORAL WILL STING, AS WILL CERTAIN KINDS OF ALGAE. DON'T PET THE SEA UR- CHINS. THEIR SPINES ARE LIKE NEEDLES AND BARBED to BOOT. THEY GO INTO YOUR SKIN NICELY BUT WON'T COME OUT. THEY'LL EVEN PENETRATE A SWIM FIN OR A SNEAKER. THEY DISSOLVE IN TIME. EVERYONE HAS A REMEDY ~ THE LIST INCLUDES DRIPPING HOT WAX ON 'EM AND POUNDING THEM WITH, SAY, A BOTTLE TO HELP THEM BREAK UP. THE BEST THING TO DO IS LEAVE THEM ALONE. IF THEY FESTER, THEY'LL COME OUT — IF NOT, THEY'LL DISSOLVE.

WHEN UNDER WAY, A FISHING LINE IS DRAGGED FROM THE STERN. ANY SURFACE-FEEDING FISH MAY BE CAUGHT ~ SPANISH MACKEREL KINGFISH, TUNA, A DOL- PHIN IF WE'RE (SIERRA)

LUCKY ---

TUNA

THEY ARE GOOD

EATING. OFTEN A BARRA— —CUDA TAKES THE LURE AND

THOSE

KINGFISH

WE

GIVE BACK TO FATHER NEPTUNE. BARRACUDAS ARE SOMETIMES POISONOUS IN THE TROPICS, AND THOUGH ISLAND- ERS WILL EAT SMALL ONES, ITS BEST NOT TO TEMPT FATE.

*Seviche* - USE FIRM WHITE FISH ~ SPANISH MACKEREL, KINGFISH, DOLPHIN. SCRAPE OR CHOP RAW FISH INTO A BOWL. COVER WITH LIME JUICE AND LET SOAK AT LEAST 3 HRS. FOR 2 C FISH, CHOP ½ MEDIUM ONION, ½ GREEN PEPPER, 1 TOMATO. ADD TO DRAINED FISH. SPRINKLE WITH PEPPER, SALT AND A LITTLE HOT SAUCE.

BARRACUDA

SERVE WITH CRACKERS.

YOU MAY ADD A LITTLE CHOPPED FRESH COCONUT OR CUCUMBER IF YOU WISH.

44

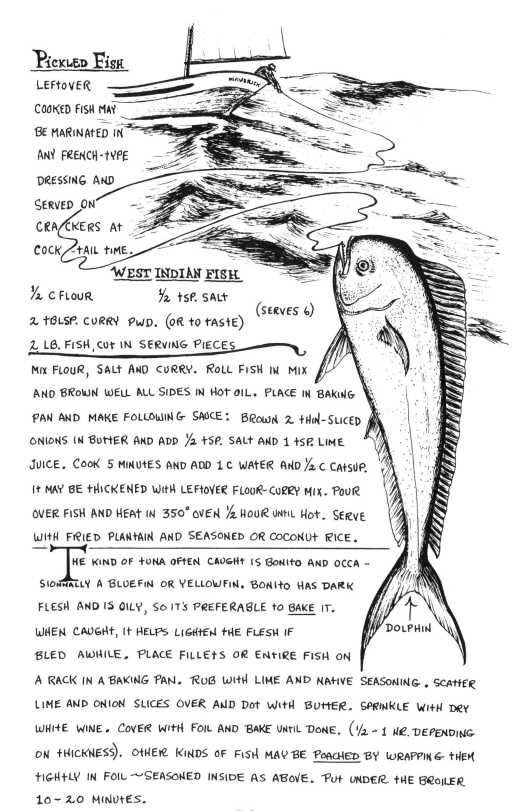

# Pickled Fish

LEFTOVER COOKED FISH MAY BE MARINATED IN ANY FRENCH-TYPE DRESSING AND SERVED ON CRACKERS AT COCK-TAIL TIME.

## WEST INDIAN FISH

½ C FLOUR ½ tSP. SALT

2 tBLSP. CURRY PWD. (OR tO tASte) (SERVES 6)

2 LB. FISH, CUt IN SERVING PIECES

MIX FLOUR, SALT AND CURRY. ROLL FISH IN MIX AND BROWN WELL ALL SIDES IN HOT OIL. PLACE IN BAKING PAN AND MAKE FOLLOWING SAUCE: BROWN 2 tHIN-SLICED ONIONS IN BUtteR AND ADD ½ tSP. SALT AND 1 tSP. LIME JUICE. COOK 5 MINUteS AND ADD 1 C WATER AND ½ C CAtSUP. It MAY BE tHICKENED WITH LEFTOVER FLOUR-CURRY MIX. POUR OVER FISH AND HEAT IN 350° OVEN ½ HOUR UNtIL HOt. SERVE WITH FRIED PLANtAIN AND SEASONED OR COCONUt RICE.

THE KIND OF tUNA OFteN CAUGHt IS BONItO AND OCCA-SIONNALLY A BLUEFIN OR YELLOWFIN. BONItO HAS DARK FLESH AND IS OILY, SO It'S PREFERABLE tO BAKE IT. WHEN CAUGHt, It HELPS LIGHTEN tHE FLESH IF BLED AWHILE. PLACE FILLEtS OR ENtIRE FISH ON A RACK IN A BAKING PAN. RUB WITH LIME AND NAtIVE SEASONING. SCATTER LIME AND ONION SLICES OVER AND DOt WITH BUTTER. SPRINKLE WITH DRY WHIte WINE. COVER WITH FOIL AND BAKE UNtIL DONE. (½ - 1 HR. DEPENDING ON tHICKNESS). OtHER KINDS OF FISH MAY BE POACHED BY WRAPPING tHEM tIGHtLY IN FOIL ~ SEASONED INSIDE AS ABOVE. PUt UNDER tHE BROILER 10 - 20 MINUteS.

DOLPHIN

When anchored in a quiet cove, there's always someone who likes to bottom fish with a drop line. Perhaps there will be SNAPPER or an OLD WIFE.

(QUEEN TRIGGERFISH)

If someone catches a small fish, he may be rolled in flour, seasoned with salt, pepper, a little curry pwd. and fried until brown. He's fine at drink time with lime slices and tartare sauce.

# Other Maverick Ways With Fish

## MAVERICK FISH BAKE (SERVES 6)

1½ lb. fresh tuna or any firm fillets          3 medium tomatos, slice thin
salt and pepper          ¼ tsp. salt          ½ tsp. dry mustard
salad oil          1 c sour cream          1 tblsp. lime juice
3 potatoes, cooked and sliced          paprika
¼ c minced onion          ⅛ tsp. pepper

Sprinkle fish with salt and pepper. Sauté in oil until done. Sauté potatoes and onions. Arrange fish and potato-onion mix in a baking dish. Top with tomatos; sprinkle with salt. Combine sour cream with mustard, lime, salt and pepper. Pour over tomatoes; sprinkle with paprika. Bake at 350° - 20 minutes or till good and hot.

When the fishing luck runs out, canned tuna may be used:

## Tuna Cashew

1 - 3 oz. jar chow mein noodles          1 can (6½ oz.) chunk tuna
1 can cr. of mushroom soup          ¼ lb. cashew nuts          ¼ c minced onion
¼ c water          1 c finely diced celery          dash pepper

Heat oven to 325°. Set aside ½ c noodles. Mix rest of ingredients and place in casserole. Sprinkle ½ c noodles over the top. Bake ½ - ¾ hour. Serves 4.

# Tuna Egg Bake

| 6 EGGS | 1 tSP. MINCED PARSLEY | 1/4 tSP. PAPRIKA |
| 2 CANS CHUNK tUNA (6½ oz.) | 1 tSP. DRY MUSTARD | 1 C CRACKER CRUMBS |
| 1 SMALL CAN MUSHROOMS | 1½ tSP. SALT | 1 Qt. MILK |
| 1/3 C BUTTER | 1 tBLSP. WORCESTERSHIRE | (SERVES 8) |

BEAT EGGS UNTIL LIGHT. StIR IN tUNA, MUSHROOMS AND tHEIR LIQUOR. MELt
BUTTER AND StIR IN ALONG WITH PARSLEY, MUSTARD, SALT, WORCESTERSHIRE
AND PAPRIKA. ADD CRUMBS. StIR IN MILK. tURN INtO GREASED BAKING DISH.
BAKE At 350° ~ 50 MINUTES OR tILL SEt.

# LOBSTER

## THE SPINEY LOBSTER

FOUND IN SOUTHERN WATERS IS A VERY tASTY RELATIVE OF tHE NORTHERN VARIETY. tHOUGH
HE LACKS tHE LARGE CLAWS AND HIS CARAPACE HAS SHARP SPINES FOR PROTECTION, tHE
tAIL CONTAINS SWEEt MEAT MUCH SOUGHt AFtER. tHE NATIVES MUSt DIVE DEEPER EACH
YEAR tO FIND HIM tO SUPPLY A RISING DEMAND. CONSEQUENTLY, IF YOU'RE ON tHE
BUYING END, YOU DIVE DEEPER IN POCKEt.

LOBSTER IS StEAMED IN SEA WAtER 15 – 30 MINUtES, DEPENDING ON
SIZE. SPINEY LOBSTER HAS BEEN KNOWN tO REACH A LENGtH OF 20" OR MORE. IF
tHERE'S A SMALL AMOUNt OF LOBSTER AND YOU WANt It tO GO A LONG WAY, tRY
tHIS SPREAD : MELt 2 tBLSP. BUttER AND SAUtÉ 1 tBLSP. CHOPPED GREEN PEPPER
AND 1 tBLSP. MINCED ONION. ADD 2 tSP. WORCESTERSHIRE, ½ tSP. SOY, 1 tSP.
CAtSUP. ADD CUt-UP COOKED LOBSTER AND SIMMER A FEW MINUtES. REMOVE FROM
FIRE AND ADD 2 tBLSP. FLOUR tO tHICKEN. REtURN tO FIRE AND COOK A FEW MIN-
UtES MORE. ADD A SMALL AMOUNt OF WAtER OR CHICKEN BROtH FOR PROPER CON-
SIStENCY. ADD A LITtLE CHOPPED tOMAtO IF YOU HAVE SOME. It'S INtERESTING
tO ADD A tOUCH OF CURRY PWD. OR HOt SAUCE, IF YOU LIKE.

WHEN tHERE ARE A FEW LOBSTERS, tHERMADOR IS A FAVORITE. It'S USUALLY
SERVED OVER RICE, OR tHE FOLLOWING CASSEROLE MAY DO.

# LOBSTER CASSEROLE

FRY 5 CHOPPED ONIONS, 4 CHOPPED GREEN PEPPERS,

↑SPOTTED EEL

2 LARGE CANS (6 OZ.) MUSHROOMS, DRAINED — IN BUTTER FOR 5 MINUTES. SPREAD IN 2 BUTTERED BAKING PANS (9 X 12 X 2). BREAK UP 4 C SOFT BREAD CRUMBS FOR EACH PAN. SPREAD OVER VEGETABLES. CUT UP COOKED LOBSTER MEAT (FROM 4 OR 5 LOBSTERS) AND SCATTER OVER BREAD. MAKE SAUCE: MELT ⅔ C BUTTER, REMOVE FROM HEAT AND ADD 1 C FLOUR. SLOWLY STIR IN 1½ QT. MILK. RETURN TO HEAT AND COOK, STIRRING, TILL SAUCE THICKENS. ADD CANNED EVAPORATED MILK TO MAKE PROPER CONSISTENCY FOR A MEDIUM CREAM SAUCE. ADD SEASONINGS — 1 TSP. CAYENNE, 1 TSP. DRY MUSTARD, SALT AND PEPPER TO TASTE, 3 TBLSP. WORCESTERSHIRE, ¼ C PARSLEY AND, AT THE LAST MINUTE, ¼ C SHERRY. POUR OVER LOBSTER, SPRINKLE WITH DRY CRUMBS AND DOT WITH BUTTER. BAKE AT 350° ABOUT ½ HR. OR TILL BUBBLING HOT.    SERVES 20.

## COCONUT LOBSTER

IS AN INTERESTING BLEND OF FLAVORS. MAKE A SAUCE BY MIXING 1 TBLSP. CORNSTARCH WITH ¼ C COLD MILK AND ½ TSP. SALT. SCALD 1¼ C MILK AND ½ C COCONUT CREAM. ADD CORNSTARCH MIX; COOK AND STIR TILL THICK. AFTER STEAMING LOBSTER, SPLIT THEM IN HALF AND REMOVE TAIL MEAT. CUT IN CHUNKS, MIX WITH SAUCE AND PILE BACK IN SHELLS TO SERVE. REHEAT IN A MODERATE OVEN IF YOU WISH.  — ENOUGH SAUCE FOR 2 LOBSTERS. GARNISH TOPS WITH PARSLEY.

## Best of all

— IS THE EASIEST. AFTER STEAMING, THE TAILS ARE BROKEN OFF AND CUT IN HALF LENGTHWISE. LAY THEM OUT IN THE BROILER PAN. BRUSH WITH LIME JUICE, BUTTER AND PEPPER. BROIL UNTIL GOOD AND HOT AND THE TOPS SLIGHTLY BROWN. THE HEADS AND BODIES MAY BE PICKED AND THE MEAT SAVED FOR SALAD AND/OR COCKTAILS. IT'S NICE TO GIVE FOLKS A CRACK AT OPENING THE LEGS AT DRINK TIME.

48

# SHRIMP

THERE IS NO SHRIMPING IN THIS PART OF THE CARIBBEAN —

But, IF THE PRICE IS RIGHT, FROZEN SHRIMP IS PURCHASED AND WE ENJOY—

## FERNANDO'S SHRIMP CREOLE

SIMMER 1½ ~ 2 LB. RAW SHRIMP WITH A CHOPPED ONION, 1 tSP. SALT AND A FEW CELERY LEAVES IN WATER TO COVER FOR 5 MINUTES. DRAIN. SAUTÉ 2 CHOPPED ONIONS, 2 CHOPPED GREEN PEPPERS AND 4 STALKS COARSELY CHOPPED CELERY IN ¼ C OIL. ADD ¼ C FLOUR, 2 tBLSP. SUGAR, SALT TO TASTE, A DASH OF CAYENNE, BLACK PEPPER, 1 CAN (#2½) TOMATOS, 1 tBLSP. WORCESTERSHIRE, AND 2 tBLSP. CHILI PWD. STIR IN THE SHRIMP AND SERVE OVER RICE. PEAS MAY BE ADDED OR SERVED ON THE SIDE.

(SERVES 8)

(SERVES 6 FOR LUNCH) ## SHRIMP QUICHE (SERVES 10 AS AN APPETIZER)

PASTRY FOR A 9" PIE SHELL

1–8 oz. PKG FROZEN, CLEANED SHRIMP

8 oz. SWISS CHEESE, GRATED

1 tBLSP. FLOUR

3 EGGS

A DASH OF CAYENNE

1 C EVAPORATED MILK

½ tSP. SALT

¼ tSP. PEPPER

CHILL PASTRY SHELL. CHOP SHRIMP. TOSS CHEESE AND FLOUR. BEAT TOGETHER EGGS, MILK, SALT, PEPPER AND CAYENNE. SPREAD ¾ OF CHEESE IN PASTRY SHELL. ADD SHRIMP AND COVER WITH REST OF CHEESE. POUR EGG MIX OVER ALL. BAKE AT 400° ~ 15 MINUTES. REDUCE HEAT TO 325° AND BAKE 40 MINUTES OR UNTIL SET. LET STAND 10 MINUTES ~ THEN CUT.

49

# Native Seasoning

EVERYONE KNOWS THAT SALT PRESERVES. IN THE WEST INDIES, LONG BEFORE COMMERCIAL SEA-SONINGS WERE AVAILABLE, PEOPLE MADE UP THEIR OWN COMBINATIONS OF HERBS AND SEASONINGS. THEY MIXED THEM WITH SALT AND KEPT THEM TO FLAVOR MEATS, FISH, SOUPS OR WHATEVER THEY FANCIED. WHEN MAVERICK STOPS AT SALT ISLAND IN THE BRITISH VIRGIN ISLANDS, A FEW POUNDS OF ROUGH-TEXTURED SALT ARE PURCHASED FROM THE LOCALS. THEY STILL HARVEST IT FROM THE SALT POND BEHIND THE VILLAGE. IT'S PER-FECT FOR CURING STAR FISH AND TO MAKE:

## SEASONED SALT — TABLE SALT MAY BE USED.

GRIND THE FOLLOWING IN A MORTAR AND PESTLE:

| | | |
|---|---|---|
| ½ C SALT | 1 STALK CELERY (LEAVES – YES) | ¼ TSP. CLOVES |
| 2 CUT UP CLOVES GARLIC | 1 SPRIG PARSLEY | ½ TSP. NUTMEG |
| ½ CUT UP MEDIUM ONION | 2 TSP. GROUND BLACK PEPPER | ¼ TSP. THYME |

GRIND ALL TOGETHER UNTIL WELL MIXED AND MOIST. IT WILL KEEP INDEFINIT-ELY IN A JAR ON THE SHELF.

## EACH ISLAND HAS A NATIVE

MARKET PLACE AND SATURDAY IS THE BIG DAY! FOLKS BRING PRODUCE IN FROM THE COUNTRY TO THE CENTER OF TOWN OR CITY AND IT'S A COLOR-FUL SCENE FULL OF ACTIVITY, BARGAINING AND BUSINESS. THERE IS AS MUCH VISITING AND GOSSIPING AS BUSINESS SOMETIMES. THERE ARE FAMILIAR AND STRANGE FRUITS AND VEGETABLES PILED UP IN GREAT ABUNDANCE. THE LARGER ISLANDS GROW A LOT OF HERBS AND SPICE AND IN THOSE MAR-KETS, THE SCENT OF CINNAMON, NUTMEG, CLOVES AND VANILLA HOVERS ABOVE THE MORE EARTHY ODORS.

# Spices and Herbs

Found in native markets : ① tied bunches of herb bouquet. Sprigs of celery, thyme, parsley chives and sage for use in stews and soups. ② Bay — (laurel) leaves — dark, fresh dried and pungent. → ③ Small, sweet peppers and smaller still very hot ones.

④ Ginger root → — boiled, the juice from this small root is used in curries and stews. Grated or preserved, it is used in cakes, cookies, candy or chutney. ⑤ Bitter chocolate — the beans have been roasted, ground and formed into rolls or balls for future use.

⑥ Long, fragrant vanilla beans, carefully wrapped.

⑦ Rolls of cinnamon bark — tied with a whisp of straw.

⑧ Baskets or trays of cloves ⑨ Allspice

⑩ Nutmeg, with their threads of bright scarlet ⑪ Mace still clinging to the outside of the nutmeg shell.

Nutmeg has so much more flavor when freshly grated for all kinds of dishes, desserts and drinks. Many of the RUM drinks and punches are made special by that dusting of fresh nutmeg. So, finally — that brings us to —

51

# Demon Rum or Kill Devil

AS RUM IS SOMETIMES KNOWN IN THE ISLANDS

A NEW ZEALAND FRIEND CALLS RUM

NELSON'S BLOOD!

DURING COLONIAL DAYS IN THE WEST INDIES, WHEREVER SUGAR CANE WAS GROWN, MOLASSES AND RUM WERE VALUABLE END PRODUCTS. THE SUGAR WENT TO ENGLAND. THE RUM WAS FOR HOME CONSUMPTION OR FOR SHIPMENT TO THE AMERICAN COLONIES ALONG WITH THE MOLASSES OUTPUT. MOLASSES KEPT THE NEW ENGLAND DISTILLERIES GOING. NORTH AMERICAN RUM OFTEN WENT THEN TO AFRICA TO BE TRADED FOR SLAVES, AND THE SLAVES WERE BROUGHT TO THE WEST INDIES TO HELP GROW MORE CANE TO MAKE MORE SUGAR, RUM AND MOLASSES ~ THE INFAMOUS TRIANGLE TRADE ON WHICH MOST OF THE ISLANDS FLOURISHED. FRESH SQUEEZED CANE JUICE IS BOILED DOWN TO MAKE MUSCOVADO, THE RAW SUGAR STILL AVAILABLE IN THE CARIBBEAN - - - - THE DRIPPINGS BECOME MOLASSES. MOLASSES IS THE BASE FOR RUM. A CLEAR WHITE RUM CAN ALSO BE MADE DIRECTLY FROM PURE CANE JUICE. Rum SEEMS TO BE THE VERY ESSENCE OF THE CARIBBEAN. IT COMES IN ALL DIFFERENT SHADES FROM LIGHT, MELLOW AND GOLDEN TO DARK BROWN, HEAVY WITH MOLASSES. EVERY ISLAND HAS IT'S FAVORITE RUM DRINK, AND IT IS ESPECIALLY PLEASING WHEN COMBINED WITH FRUIT.

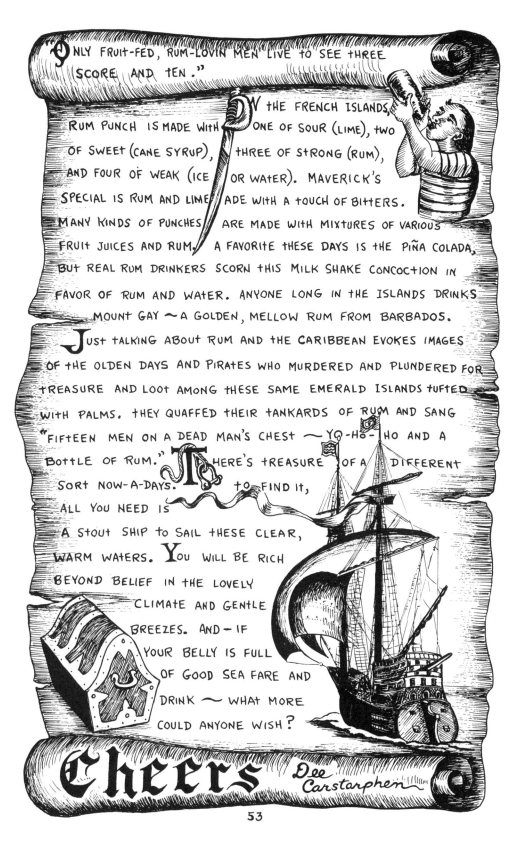

"ONLY FRUIT-FED, RUM-LOVIN MEN LIVE TO SEE THREE SCORE AND TEN."

NOW THE FRENCH ISLANDS, RUM PUNCH IS MADE WITH ONE OF SOUR (LIME), TWO OF SWEET (CANE SYRUP), THREE OF STRONG (RUM), AND FOUR OF WEAK (ICE OR WATER). MAVERICK'S SPECIAL IS RUM AND LIMEADE WITH A TOUCH OF BITTERS. MANY KINDS OF PUNCHES ARE MADE WITH MIXTURES OF VARIOUS FRUIT JUICES AND RUM. A FAVORITE THESE DAYS IS THE PIÑA COLADA, BUT REAL RUM DRINKERS SCORN THIS MILK SHAKE CONCOCTION IN FAVOR OF RUM AND WATER. ANYONE LONG IN THE ISLANDS DRINKS MOUNT GAY ~ A GOLDEN, MELLOW RUM FROM BARBADOS.

JUST TALKING ABOUT RUM AND THE CARIBBEAN EVOKES IMAGES OF THE OLDEN DAYS AND PIRATES WHO MURDERED AND PLUNDERED FOR TREASURE AND LOOT AMONG THESE SAME EMERALD ISLANDS TUFTED WITH PALMS. THEY QUAFFED THEIR TANKARDS OF RUM AND SANG "FIFTEEN MEN ON A DEAD MAN'S CHEST ~ YO-HO-HO AND A BOTTLE OF RUM." THERE'S TREASURE OF A DIFFERENT SORT NOW-A-DAYS. TO FIND IT, ALL YOU NEED IS A STOUT SHIP TO SAIL THESE CLEAR, WARM WATERS. YOU WILL BE RICH BEYOND BELIEF IN THE LOVELY CLIMATE AND GENTLE BREEZES. AND — IF YOUR BELLY IS FULL OF GOOD SEA FARE AND DRINK ~ WHAT MORE COULD ANYONE WISH?

Cheers

Dee Carstarphen

# Notes

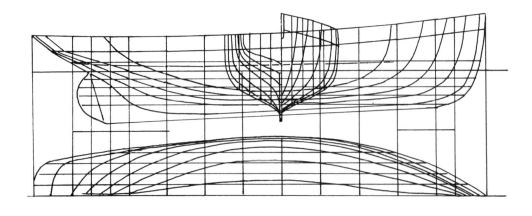

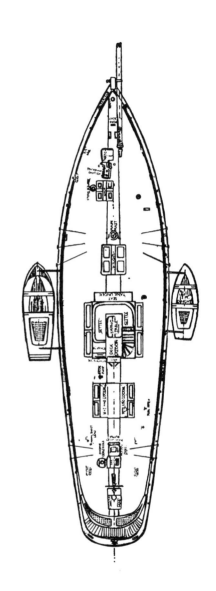

# Notes

# Notes

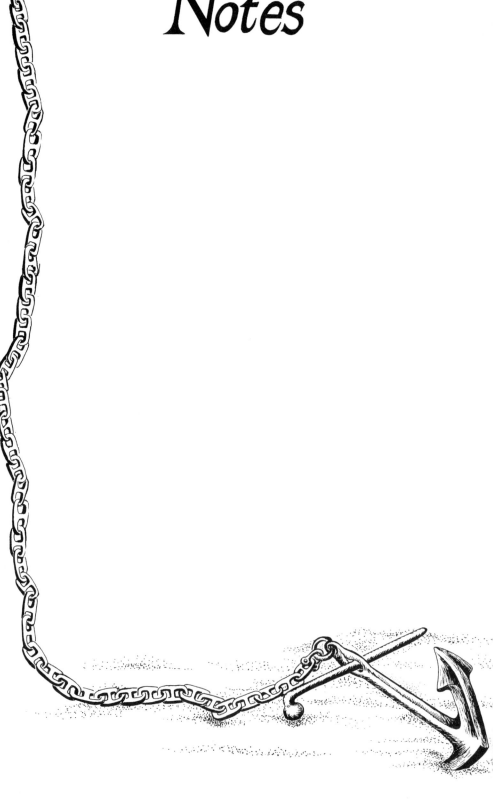